2014 Bank Lending Practices

The October 2014 Senior Loan Officer Opinion Survey on Bank Lending Practices addressed changes in the standards and terms on, and demand for, bank loans to businesses and households over the past three months.[1] This summary discusses the responses from 76 domestic banks and 22 U.S. branches and agencies of foreign banks.[2]

Regarding loans to businesses, the October survey results indicated that only a modest net fraction of banks eased their standards for commercial and industrial (C&I) loans to firms of all sizes, but generally larger net fractions of banks eased each of the pricing terms listed in the survey and some non-price terms.[3] Banks also reported having eased standards for construction and land development loans, a category of commercial real estate (CRE) loans included in the survey. On the demand side, modest net fractions of banks reported stronger demand for C&I loans to larger firms; similar net fractions experienced stronger demand for all three categories of CRE loans covered in the survey.[4]

The survey included a set of special questions on retail small business lending.[5] Banks on net reported that the volume of applications received for new retail small business loans over the past year had been close to the midpoint of its range over the past decade. Moreover, modest net fractions of banks reported that many minimum underwriting requirements for approving applications from small business owners to be somewhat tighter than the midpoint of its range. Even so, most banks expected a moderate increase in retail small business lending over the next year.

Regarding loans to households, some large banks reported having eased standards on closed-end mortgage loans, but respondents generally indicated little change in standards and terms for other types of loans to households. Reported changes in loan demand were mixed. Moderate net fractions of banks reported stronger demand for auto loans and weaker demand for nontraditional closed-end mortgage loans. Demand for other types of loans to households was about unchanged at most banks.

---

[1] Respondent banks received the survey on or after September 30, 2014, and responses were due by October 14, 2014.

[2] Unless otherwise indicated, the document refers to reports from domestic banks in the survey.

[3] For questions that ask about lending standards or terms, reported net fractions equal the fraction of banks that reported having tightened ("tightened considerably" or "tightened somewhat") minus the fraction of banks that reported having eased ("eased considerably" or "eased somewhat"). For questions that ask about loan demand, reported net fractions equal the fraction of banks that reported stronger demand ("substantially stronger" or "moderately stronger") minus the fraction of banks that reported weaker demand ("substantially weaker" or "moderately weaker").

[4] The three categories of CRE loans covered in the survey are construction and land development loans, loans secured by nonfarm nonresidential structures, and loans secured by multifamily residential properties.

[5] *Retail small business loans* are loans to small businesses evaluated with credit scores that are based on the creditworthiness of the business owner rather than the firm itself. The average size of these businesses is significantly smaller than the $50 million in annual sales normally used in the survey to define small firms.

Another set of special questions examined banks' credit policies for subprime auto loans. Very few banks reported changes in terms on subprime auto loans over the past year and most respondents anticipated that lending policies on such loans would remain about unchanged over the next year.

Lending to Businesses
(Table 1, questions 1–15; Table 2, questions 1–8)

Questions on commercial and industrial lending. A modest percentage of banks reported having eased standards on C&I loans to firms of all sizes.[6] Banks reported having eased, on net, each of the surveyed price terms on C&I loans to firms of all sizes. In particular, a large net fraction of banks eased spreads, a moderate net fraction eased the cost of credit lines and interest rate floors, and a modest net fraction eased premiums charged on riskier loans. Non-price terms generally remained about unchanged, except that modest net fractions of banks reported having eased loan covenants or having increased the maximum size of credit lines on net. Foreign banks reported having eased spreads of C&I loans over banks' cost of funds.

Most respondents that reported having eased either standards or terms on C&I loans over the past three months cited more-aggressive competition from other banks or nonbank lenders as an important reason for having done so. Smaller numbers of banks also attributed their easing to a more favorable or less uncertain economic outlook and increased tolerance for risk.

On the demand side, a modest net fraction of banks reported having experienced stronger demand for C&I loans from large and middle-market firms. A similar net fraction of banks reported a higher number of inquiries from potential business borrowers for new credit lines or increases in existing lines. Banks reported that loan demand from small firms had remained about unchanged on net. To explain the reported increase in loan demand by larger firms, banks cited a wide range of customers' financing needs, particularly those related to inventories, accounts receivable, investment in plant or equipment, and mergers or acquisitions. Foreign banks also reported having seen stronger demand on net.

Special questions on retail small business lending. The October survey contained a set of special questions on banks' retail small business lending. Banks on net reported that the volume of applications for retail small business loans received over the past year was close to the midpoint of its range over the past decade. Moreover, on balance, banks indicated that underwriting policies for approving applications for retail small business loans were somewhat tighter than the midpoint of their range over the past decade. In particular, modest net fractions of banks reported having somewhat tighter minimum underwriting requirements for the liquidity position, the quality of personal guarantees, and the debt-to-income ratio of the business owners applying for such loans. Even so, the large majority of banks expected that retail small business lending would increase moderately over the next year.

---

[6] The survey asked respondents separately about their standards for, and demand from, large and middle-market firms, which are generally defined as firms with annual sales of $50 million or more, and small firms, those with annual sales of less than $50 million.

Questions on commercial real estate lending. A modest net fraction of banks reported that they had eased standards on construction and land development loans, while standards for loans secured by nonfarm nonresidential structures and multifamily residential properties remained about unchanged. Moderate net fractions of banks indicated that they had experienced stronger demand for all three subcategories of CRE loans. On balance, foreign banks also reported having eased lending standards on CRE loans and having seen stronger demand for such loans over the past three months.

Lending to Households
(Table 1, questions 16–32)

Questions on residential real estate lending. A moderate net fraction of large banks reported that they had eased standards on prime residential mortgages over the past three months. Smaller banks reported that standards for prime residential mortgages were about unchanged on net. Reported changes in demand for mortgage loans were mixed. On net, although large banks reported that demand for prime mortgages had weakened, smaller banks experienced increases. However, demand for nontraditional mortgages was weaker, on net, across both bank size groups. Few banks reported having changed their standards on home-equity lines of credit, and respondents indicated that they had experienced little change in demand for such loans on net.

Questions on consumer lending. A small net fraction of banks indicated that they were more willing to make consumer installment loans as compared with the previous quarter. A very few banks reported having eased their standards for approving applications for credit cards, and a modest net fraction of banks indicated having eased their standards for auto loans. Most terms on credit cards were little changed, except for credit limits and required minimum credit scores, which a modest net fraction of banks reported having eased. Very few banks reported changes on any of the terms on auto loans, except for a small number of banks that had either increased or reduced the spreads of loan rates over cost of funds. Most banks reported that they had kept their standards and terms on other types of consumer loans unchanged.

A moderate fraction of banks, on net, reported having experienced an increase in demand for auto loans over the past three months. In contrast, most banks reported that demand for credit cards and other consumer loans had not significantly changed over the same period.

Special questions on subprime auto lending. A set of special questions included in this survey asked banks to describe the changes in their terms for subprime auto loans over the past year. Only 19 of the 76 banks that responded to the survey reported that they currently originate subprime auto loans. For each of the surveyed policies—such as loan rate spreads, minimum required down payments, and credit scores— most banks reported no change relative to a year ago. In addition, most of those banks anticipated that their lending policies would stay about unchanged over the next year.

This document was prepared by Vladimir Yankov, with the assistance of Kamran Gupta, Nathan Lloyd, and Shaily Patel, Division of Monetary Affairs, Board of Governors of the Federal Reserve System.

Measures of Supply and Demand for Commercial and Industrial Loans, by Size of Firm Seeking Loan

Net Percentage of Domestic Respondents Tightening Standards for Commercial and Industrial Loans

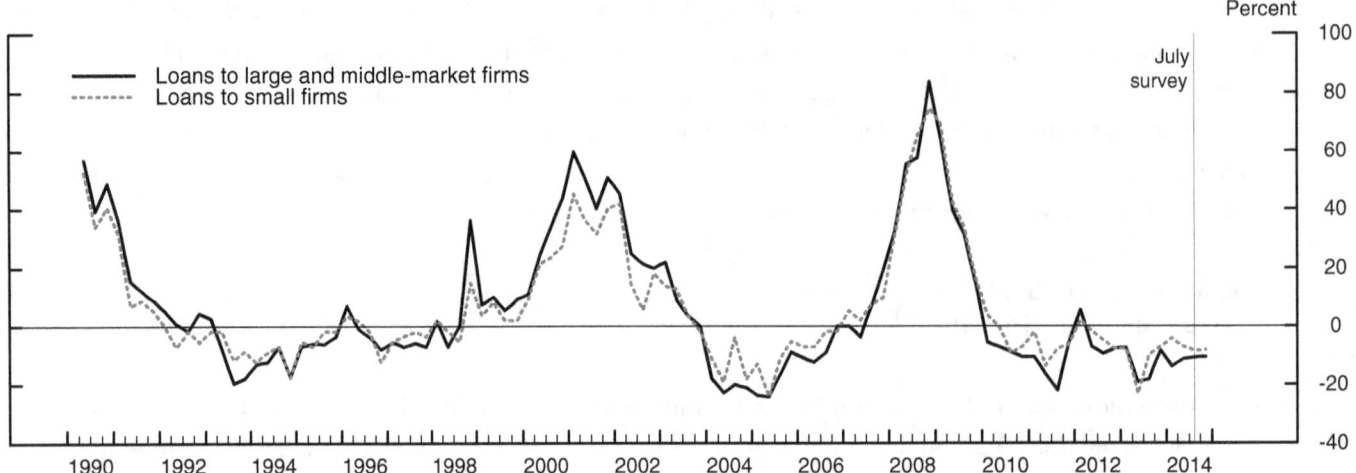

Net Percentage of Domestic Respondents Increasing Spreads of Loan Rates over Bank's Cost of Funds

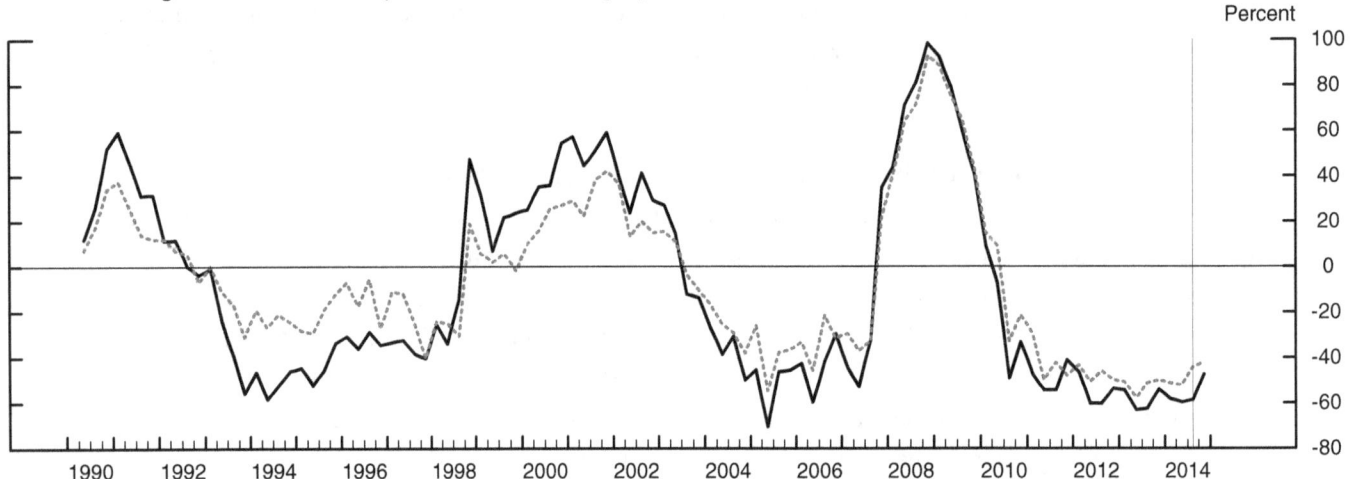

Net Percentage of Domestic Respondents Reporting Stronger Demand for Commercial and Industrial Loans

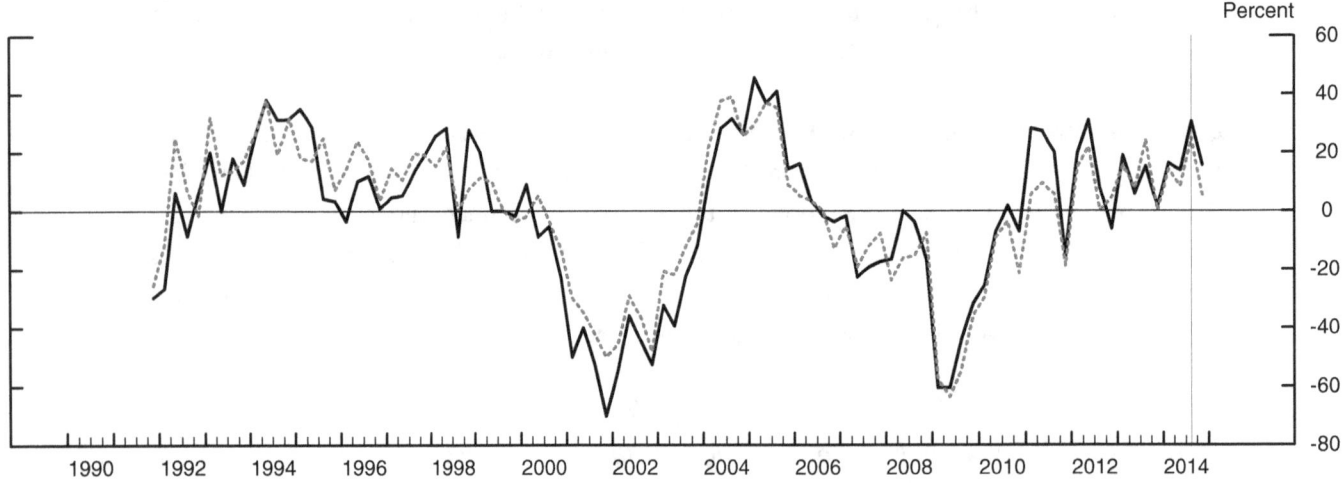

Measures of Supply and Demand for Commercial Real Estate Loans

Net Percentage of Domestic Respondents Tightening Standards for Commercial Real Estate Loans

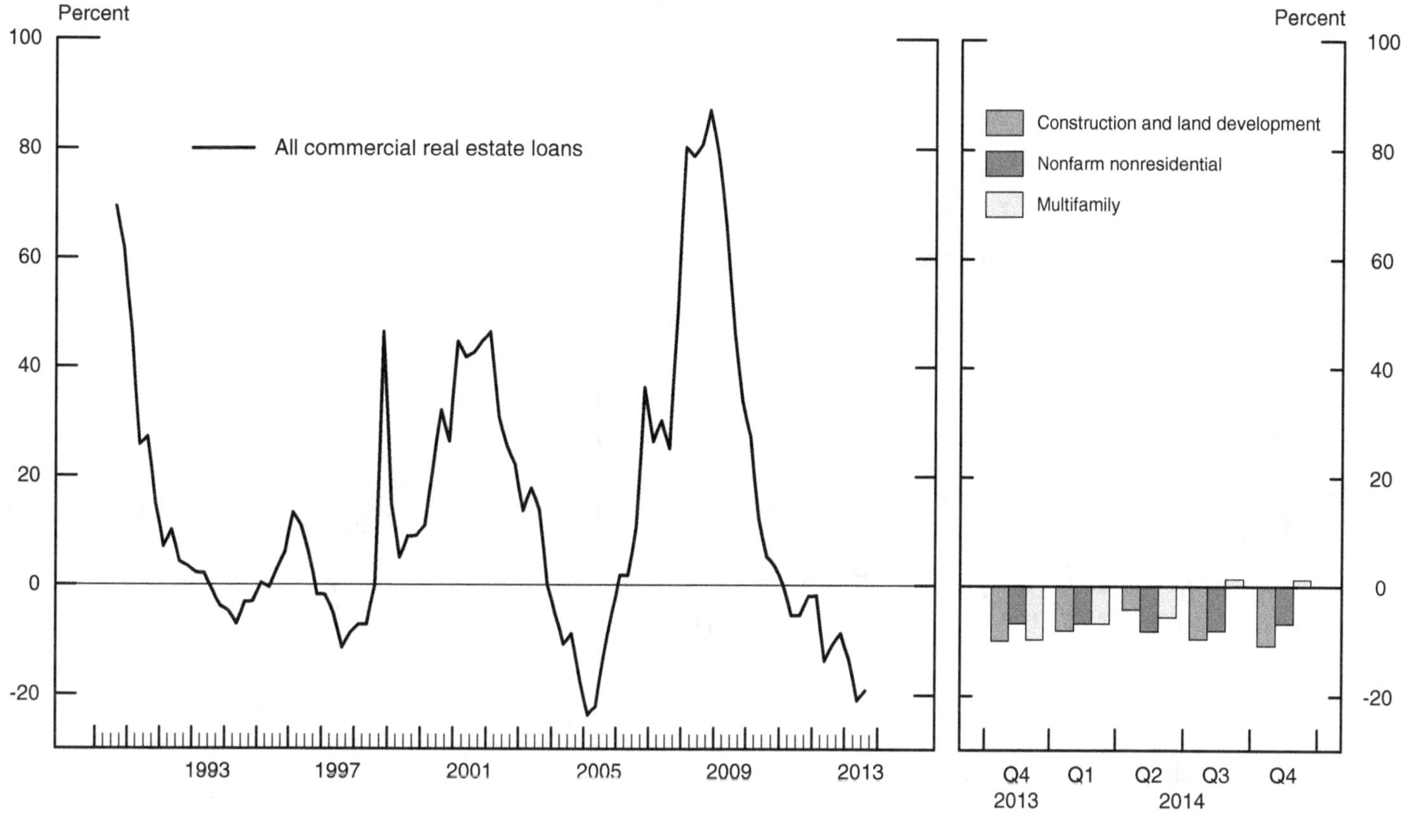

Note: For data starting in 2013:Q4, changes in standards for construction and land development, nonfarm nonresidential, and multifamily loans are reported separately.

Net Percentage of Domestic Respondents Reporting Stronger Demand for Commercial Real Estate Loans

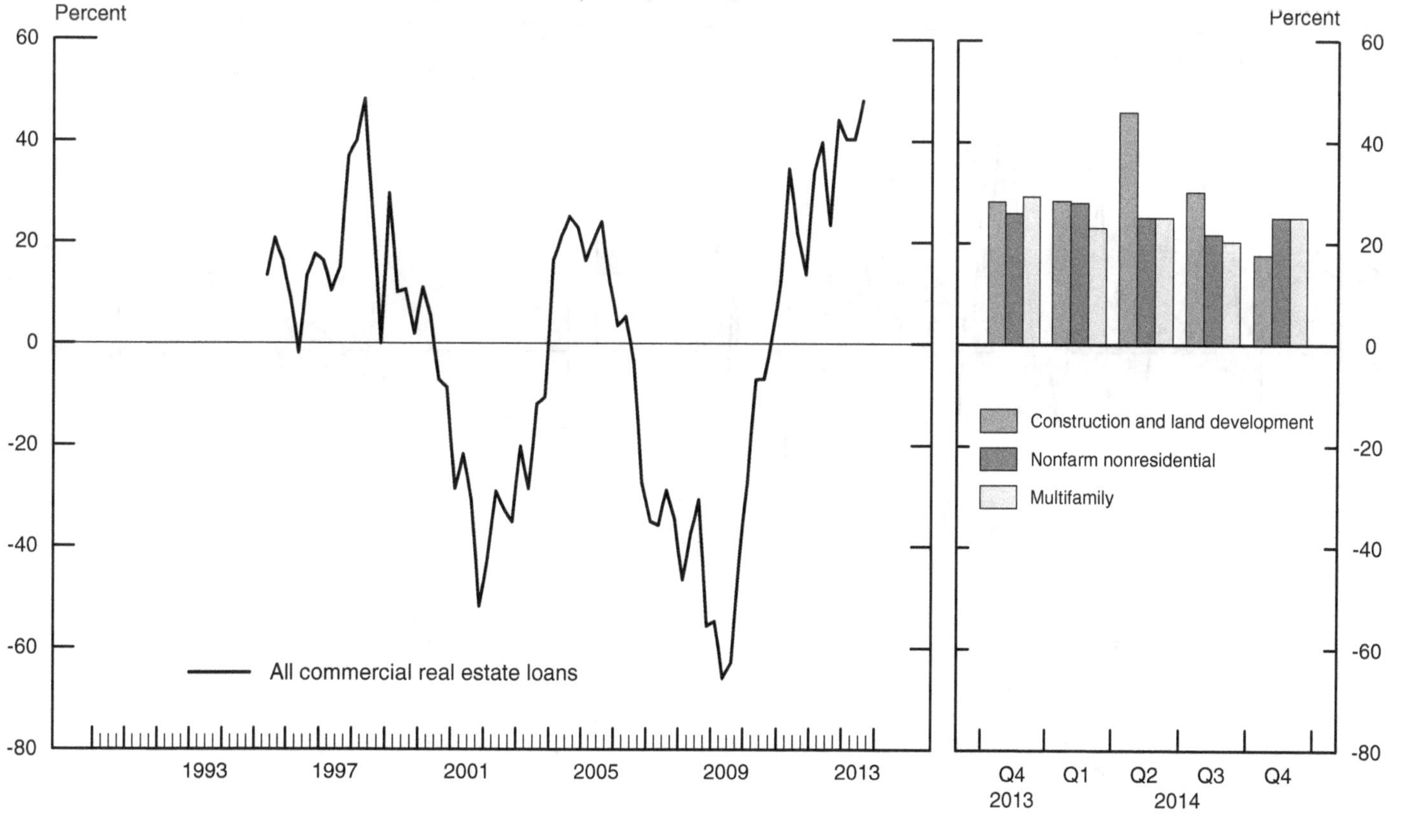

Note: For data starting in 2013:Q4, changes in demand for construction and land development, nonfarm nonresidential, and multifamily loans are reported separately.

Measures of Supply and Demand for Residential Mortgage Loans

Net Percentage of Domestic Respondents Tightening Standards for Residential Mortgage Loans

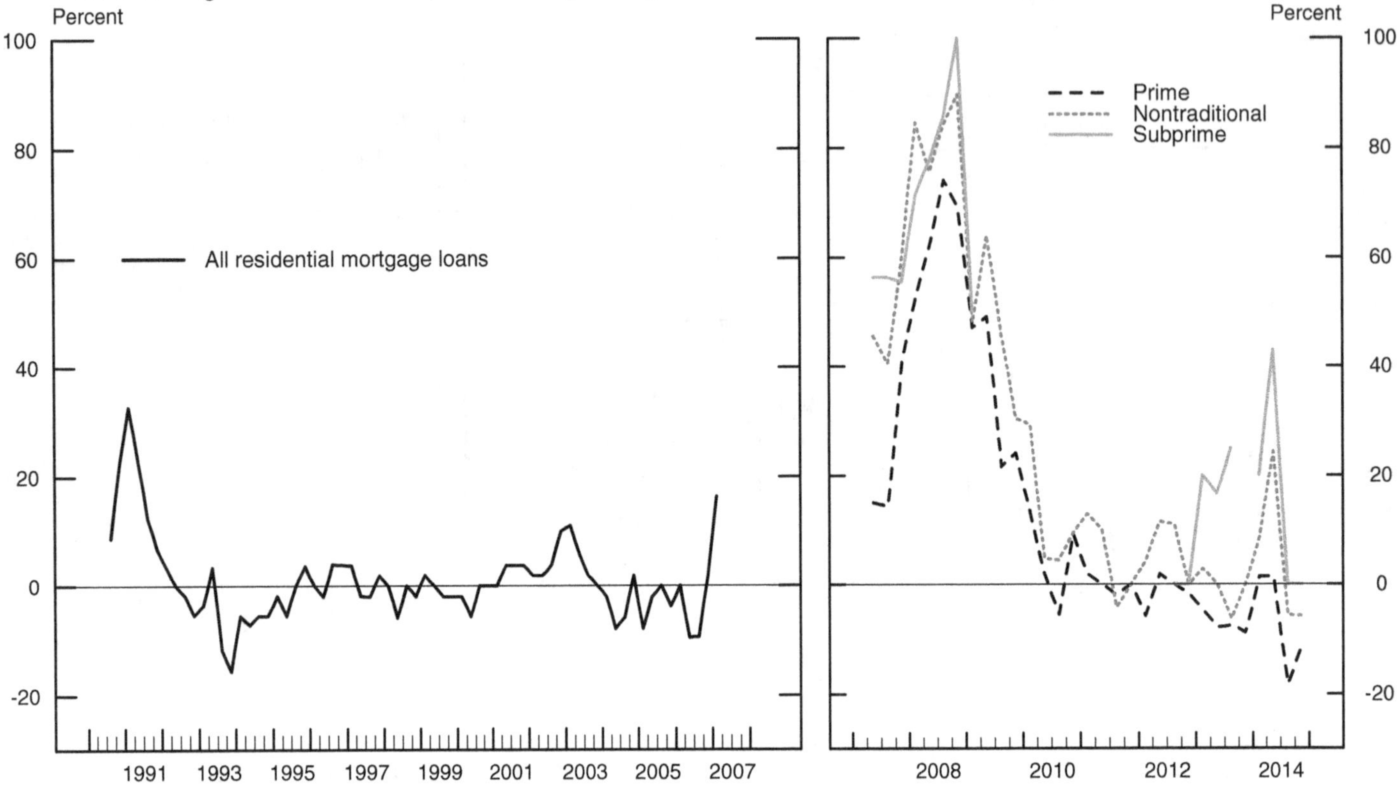

Note: For data starting in 2007:Q2, changes in standards for prime, nontraditional, and subprime mortgage loans are reported separately. Series are not reported when the number of respondents is three or fewer.

Net Percentage of Domestic Respondents Reporting Stronger Demand for Residential Mortgage Loans

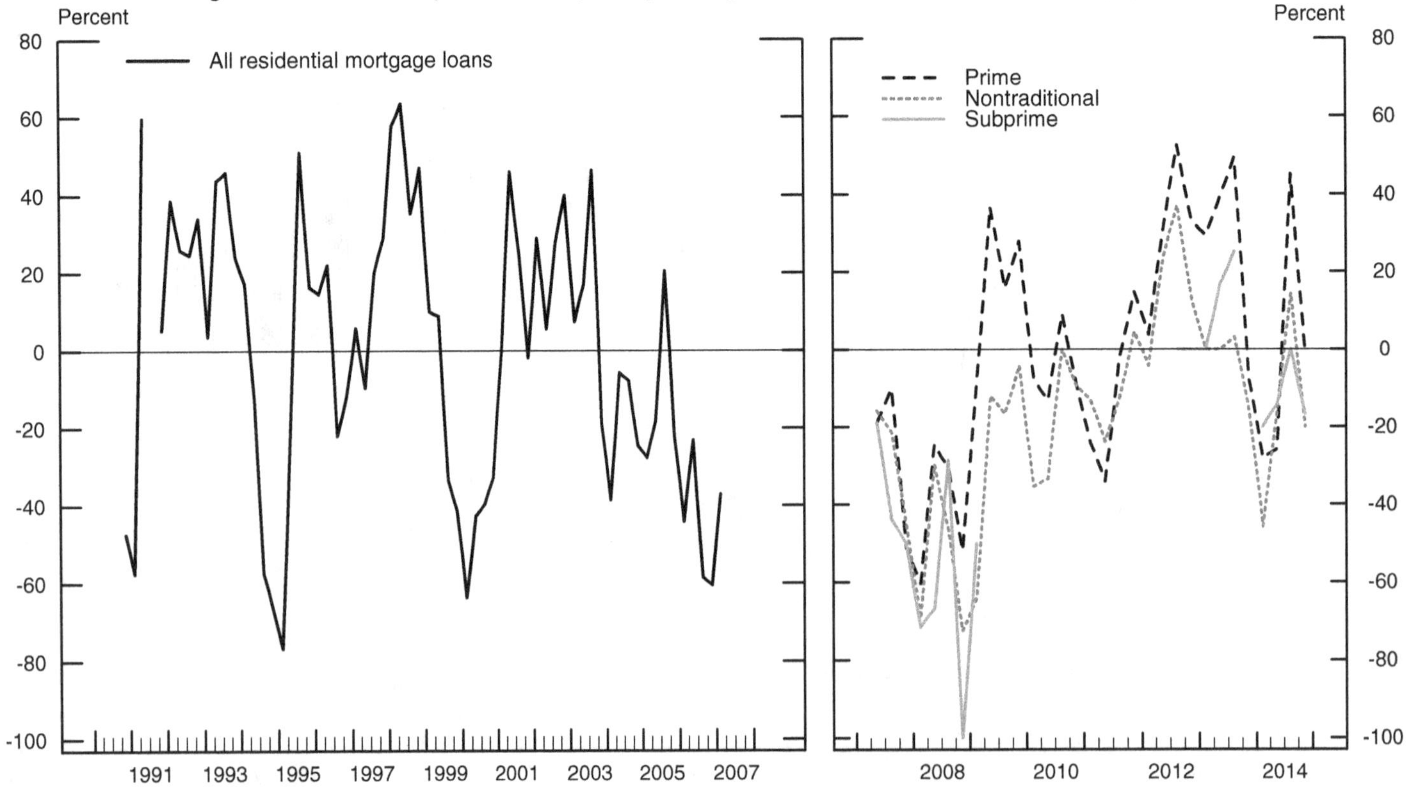

Note: For data starting in 2007:Q2, changes in demand for prime, nontraditional, and subprime mortgage loans are reported separately. Series are not reported when the number of respondents is three or fewer.

Measures of Supply and Demand for Consumer Loans

Net Percentage of Domestic Respondents Tightening Standards for Consumer Loans

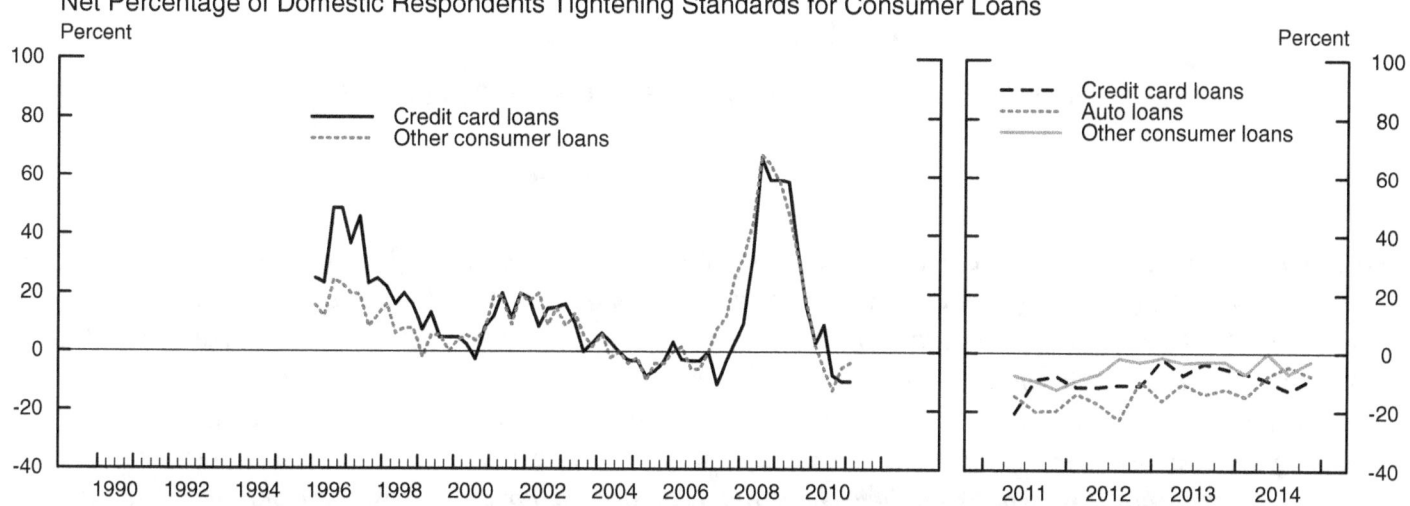

Note: For data starting in 2011:Q2, changes in standards for auto loans and consumer loans excluding credit card and auto loans are reported separately. In 2011:Q2 only, new and used auto loans are reported separately and equally weighted to calculate the auto loans series.

Net Percentage of Domestic Respondents Reporting Increased Willingness to Make Consumer Installment Loans

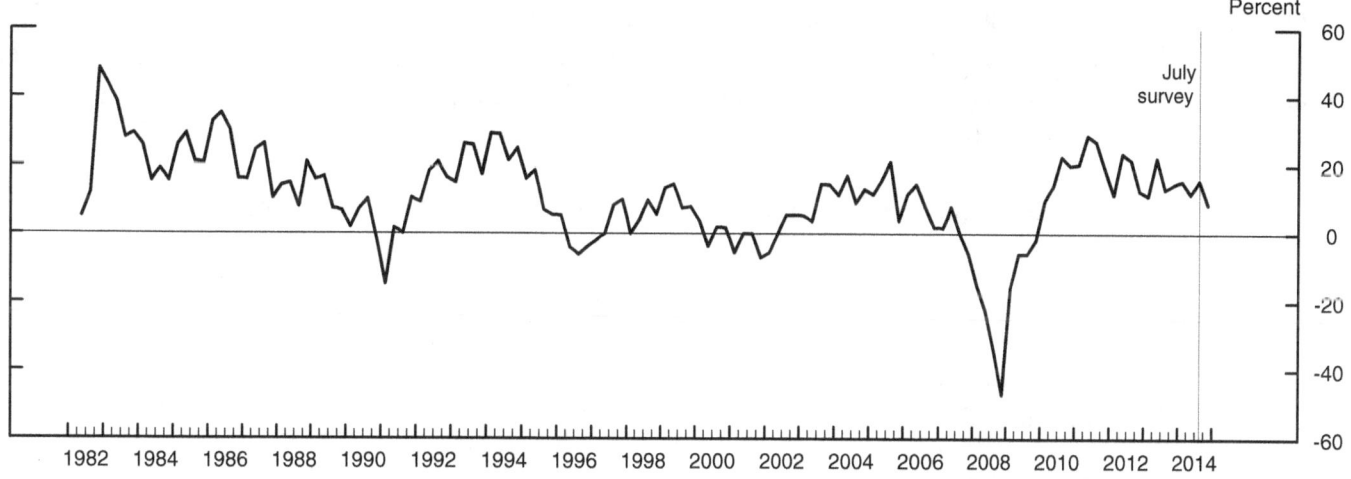

Net Percentage of Domestic Respondents Reporting Stronger Demand for Consumer Loans

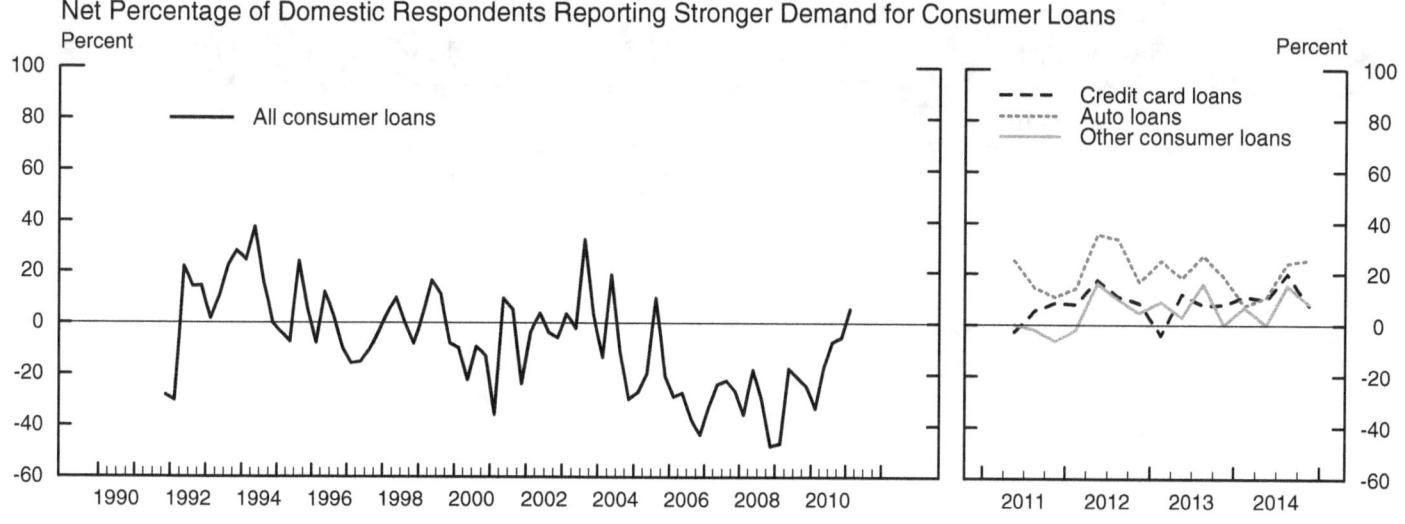

Note: For data starting in 2011:Q2, changes in demand for credit card loans, auto loans, and consumer loans excluding credit card and auto loans are reported separately.

Table 1

Senior Loan Officer Opinion Survey on Bank Lending Practices at Selected Large Banks in the United States [1]

(Status of policy as of October 2014)

Questions 1-6 ask about commercial and industrial (C&I) loans at your bank. Questions 1-3 deal with changes in your bank's lending policies over the past three months. Questions 4-5 deal with changes in demand for C&I loans over the past three months. Question 6 asks about changes in prospective demand for C&I loans at your bank, as indicated by the volume of recent inquiries about the availability of new credit lines or increases in existing lines. If your bank's lending policies have not changed over the past three months, please report them as unchanged even if the policies are either restrictive or accommodative relative to longer-term norms. If your bank's policies have tightened or eased over the past three months, please so report them regardless of how they stand relative to longer-term norms. Also, please report changes in enforcement of existing policies as changes in policies.

1. Over the past three months, how have your bank's credit standards for approving applications for C&I loans or credit lines—other than those to be used to finance mergers and acquisitions—to large and middle-market firms and to small firms changed? (If your bank defines firm size differently from the categories suggested below, please use your definitions and indicate what they are.)

A. Standards for large and middle-market firms (annual sales of $50 million or more):

	All Respondents		Large Banks		Other Banks	
	Banks	Percent	Banks	Percent	Banks	Percent
Tightened considerably	0	0.0	0	0.0	0	0.0
Tightened somewhat	0	0.0	0	0.0	0	0.0
Remained basically unchanged	68	89.5	36	90.0	32	88.9
Eased somewhat	8	10.5	4	10.0	4	11.1
Eased considerably	0	0.0	0	0.0	0	0.0
Total	76	100.0	40	100.0	36	100.0

B. Standards for small firms (annual sales of less than $50 million):

	All Respondents		Large Banks		Other Banks	
	Banks	Percent	Banks	Percent	Banks	Percent
Tightened considerably	0	0.0	0	0.0	0	0.0
Tightened somewhat	0	0.0	0	0.0	0	0.0
Remained basically unchanged	67	91.8	34	91.9	33	91.7
Eased somewhat	6	8.2	3	8.1	3	8.3
Eased considerably	0	0.0	0	0.0	0	0.0
Total	73	100.0	37	100.0	36	100.0

2. For applications for C&I loans or credit lines—other than those to be used to finance mergers and acquisitions—from large and middle-market firms and from small firms that your bank currently is willing to approve, how have the terms of those loans changed over the past three months?

A. Terms for large and middle-market firms (annual sales of $50 million or more):

a. Maximum size of credit lines

	All Respondents		Large Banks		Other Banks	
	Banks	Percent	Banks	Percent	Banks	Percent
Tightened considerably	0	0.0	0	0.0	0	0.0
Tightened somewhat	1	1.3	0	0.0	1	2.8
Remained basically unchanged	64	84.2	35	87.5	29	80.6
Eased somewhat	11	14.5	5	12.5	6	16.7
Eased considerably	0	0.0	0	0.0	0	0.0
Total	76	100.0	40	100.0	36	100.0

b. Maximum maturity of loans or credit lines

	All Respondents		Large Banks		Other Banks	
	Banks	Percent	Banks	Percent	Banks	Percent
Tightened considerably	0	0.0	0	0.0	0	0.0
Tightened somewhat	1	1.3	0	0.0	1	2.8
Remained basically unchanged	69	90.8	38	95.0	31	86.1
Eased somewhat	6	7.9	2	5.0	4	11.1
Eased considerably	0	0.0	0	0.0	0	0.0
Total	76	100.0	40	100.0	36	100.0

c. Costs of credit lines

	All Respondents		Large Banks		Other Banks	
	Banks	Percent	Banks	Percent	Banks	Percent
Tightened considerably	0	0.0	0	0.0	0	0.0
Tightened somewhat	1	1.3	1	2.5	0	0.0
Remained basically unchanged	55	72.4	29	72.5	26	72.2
Eased somewhat	19	25.0	10	25.0	9	25.0
Eased considerably	1	1.3	0	0.0	1	2.8
Total	76	100.0	40	100.0	36	100.0

d. Spreads of loan rates over your bank's cost of funds (wider spreads=tightened, narrower spreads=eased)

	All Respondents		Large Banks		Other Banks	
	Banks	Percent	Banks	Percent	Banks	Percent
Tightened considerably	0	0.0	0	0.0	0	0.0
Tightened somewhat	1	1.3	1	2.5	0	0.0
Remained basically unchanged	38	50.0	20	50.0	18	50.0
Eased somewhat	36	47.4	19	47.5	17	47.2
Eased considerably	1	1.3	0	0.0	1	2.8
Total	76	100.0	40	100.0	36	100.0

e. Premiums charged on riskier loans

	All Respondents		Large Banks		Other Banks	
	Banks	Percent	Banks	Percent	Banks	Percent
Tightened considerably	0	0.0	0	0.0	0	0.0
Tightened somewhat	0	0.0	0	0.0	0	0.0
Remained basically unchanged	66	86.8	33	82.5	33	91.7
Eased somewhat	10	13.2	7	17.5	3	8.3
Eased considerably	0	0.0	0	0.0	0	0.0
Total	76	100.0	40	100.0	36	100.0

f. Loan covenants

	All Respondents		Large Banks		Other Banks	
	Banks	Percent	Banks	Percent	Banks	Percent
Tightened considerably	0	0.0	0	0.0	0	0.0
Tightened somewhat	0	0.0	0	0.0	0	0.0
Remained basically unchanged	61	80.3	30	75.0	31	86.1
Eased somewhat	15	19.7	10	25.0	5	13.9
Eased considerably	0	0.0	0	0.0	0	0.0
Total	76	100.0	40	100.0	36	100.0

g. Collateralization requirements

	All Respondents		Large Banks		Other Banks	
	Banks	Percent	Banks	Percent	Banks	Percent
Tightened considerably	0	0.0	0	0.0	0	0.0
Tightened somewhat	0	0.0	0	0.0	0	0.0
Remained basically unchanged	73	96.1	39	97.5	34	94.4
Eased somewhat	3	3.9	1	2.5	2	5.6
Eased considerably	0	0.0	0	0.0	0	0.0
Total	76	100.0	40	100.0	36	100.0

h. Use of interest rate floors (more use=tightened, less use=eased)

	All Respondents		Large Banks		Other Banks	
	Banks	Percent	Banks	Percent	Banks	Percent
Tightened considerably	0	0.0	0	0.0	0	0.0
Tightened somewhat	0	0.0	0	0.0	0	0.0
Remained basically unchanged	55	73.3	30	76.9	25	69.4
Eased somewhat	14	18.7	7	17.9	7	19.4
Eased considerably	6	8.0	2	5.1	4	11.1
Total	75	100.0	39	100.0	36	100.0

B. Terms for small firms (annual sales of less than $50 million):

a. Maximum size of credit lines

	All Respondents		Large Banks		Other Banks	
	Banks	Percent	Banks	Percent	Banks	Percent
Tightened considerably	0	0.0	0	0.0	0	0.0
Tightened somewhat	0	0.0	0	0.0	0	0.0
Remained basically unchanged	66	91.7	35	94.6	31	88.6
Eased somewhat	6	8.3	2	5.4	4	11.4
Eased considerably	0	0.0	0	0.0	0	0.0
Total	72	100.0	37	100.0	35	100.0

b. Maximum maturity of loans or credit lines

	All Respondents		Large Banks		Other Banks	
	Banks	Percent	Banks	Percent	Banks	Percent
Tightened considerably	0	0.0	0	0.0	0	0.0
Tightened somewhat	1	1.4	0	0.0	1	2.9
Remained basically unchanged	63	87.5	34	91.9	29	82.9
Eased somewhat	8	11.1	3	8.1	5	14.3
Eased considerably	0	0.0	0	0.0	0	0.0
Total	72	100.0	37	100.0	35	100.0

c. Costs of credit lines

	All Respondents		Large Banks		Other Banks	
	Banks	Percent	Banks	Percent	Banks	Percent
Tightened considerably	0	0.0	0	0.0	0	0.0
Tightened somewhat	1	1.4	1	2.7	0	0.0
Remained basically unchanged	57	79.2	28	75.7	29	82.9
Eased somewhat	14	19.4	8	21.6	6	17.1
Eased considerably	0	0.0	0	0.0	0	0.0
Total	72	100.0	37	100.0	35	100.0

d. Spreads of loan rates over your bank's cost of funds (wider spreads=tightened, narrower spreads=eased)

	All Respondents		Large Banks		Other Banks	
	Banks	Percent	Banks	Percent	Banks	Percent
Tightened considerably	0	0.0	0	0.0	0	0.0
Tightened somewhat	2	2.8	2	5.4	0	0.0
Remained basically unchanged	38	52.8	18	48.6	20	57.1
Eased somewhat	32	44.4	17	45.9	15	42.9
Eased considerably	0	0.0	0	0.0	0	0.0
Total	72	100.0	37	100.0	35	100.0

e. Premiums charged on riskier loans

	All Respondents		Large Banks		Other Banks	
	Banks	Percent	Banks	Percent	Banks	Percent
Tightened considerably	0	0.0	0	0.0	0	0.0
Tightened somewhat	0	0.0	0	0.0	0	0.0
Remained basically unchanged	63	87.5	32	86.5	31	88.6
Eased somewhat	9	12.5	5	13.5	4	11.4
Eased considerably	0	0.0	0	0.0	0	0.0
Total	72	100.0	37	100.0	35	100.0

f. Loan covenants

	All Respondents		Large Banks		Other Banks	
	Banks	Percent	Banks	Percent	Banks	Percent
Tightened considerably	0	0.0	0	0.0	0	0.0
Tightened somewhat	0	0.0	0	0.0	0	0.0
Remained basically unchanged	60	83.3	32	86.5	28	80.0
Eased somewhat	12	16.7	5	13.5	7	20.0
Eased considerably	0	0.0	0	0.0	0	0.0
Total	72	100.0	37	100.0	35	100.0

g. Collateralization requirements

	All Respondents		Large Banks		Other Banks	
	Banks	Percent	Banks	Percent	Banks	Percent
Tightened considerably	0	0.0	0	0.0	0	0.0
Tightened somewhat	0	0.0	0	0.0	0	0.0
Remained basically unchanged	68	94.4	36	97.3	32	91.4
Eased somewhat	4	5.6	1	2.7	3	8.6
Eased considerably	0	0.0	0	0.0	0	0.0
Total	72	100.0	37	100.0	35	100.0

h. Use of interest rate floors (more use=tightened, less use=eased)

	All Respondents		Large Banks		Other Banks	
	Banks	Percent	Banks	Percent	Banks	Percent
Tightened considerably	0	0.0	0	0.0	0	0.0
Tightened somewhat	0	0.0	0	0.0	0	0.0
Remained basically unchanged	54	76.1	29	80.6	25	71.4
Eased somewhat	13	18.3	5	13.9	8	22.9
Eased considerably	4	5.6	2	5.6	2	5.7
Total	71	100.0	36	100.0	35	100.0

3. If your bank has tightened or eased its credit standards or its terms for C&I loans or credit lines over the past three months (as described in questions 1 and 2), how important have been the following possible reasons for the change?

A. Possible reasons for tightening credit standards or loan terms:

a. Deterioration in your bank's current or expected capital position

	All Respondents		Large Banks		Other Banks	
	Banks	Percent	Banks	Percent	Banks	Percent
Not important	5	100.0	2	100.0	3	100.0
Somewhat important	0	0.0	0	0.0	0	0.0
Very important	0	0.0	0	0.0	0	0.0
Total	5	100.0	2	100.0	3	100.0

b. Less favorable or more uncertain economic outlook

	All Respondents		Large Banks		Other Banks	
	Banks	Percent	Banks	Percent	Banks	Percent
Not important	4	80.0	1	50.0	3	100.0
Somewhat important	1	20.0	1	50.0	0	0.0
Very important	0	0.0	0	0.0	0	0.0
Total	5	100.0	2	100.0	3	100.0

c. Worsening of industry-specific problems (please specify industries)

	All Respondents		Large Banks		Other Banks	
	Banks	Percent	Banks	Percent	Banks	Percent
Not important	4	80.0	2	100.0	2	66.7
Somewhat important	1	20.0	0	0.0	1	33.3
Very important	0	0.0	0	0.0	0	0.0
Total	5	100.0	2	100.0	3	100.0

d. Less aggressive competition from other banks or nonbank lenders (other financial intermediaries or the capital markets)

	All Respondents		Large Banks		Other Banks	
	Banks	Percent	Banks	Percent	Banks	Percent
Not important	5	100.0	2	100.0	3	100.0
Somewhat important	0	0.0	0	0.0	0	0.0
Very important	0	0.0	0	0.0	0	0.0
Total	5	100.0	2	100.0	3	100.0

e. Reduced tolerance for risk

	All Respondents		Large Banks		Other Banks	
	Banks	Percent	Banks	Percent	Banks	Percent
Not important	3	60.0	1	50.0	2	66.7
Somewhat important	2	40.0	1	50.0	1	33.3
Very important	0	0.0	0	0.0	0	0.0
Total	5	100.0	2	100.0	3	100.0

f. Decreased liquidity in the secondary market for these loans

	All Respondents		Large Banks		Other Banks	
	Banks	Percent	Banks	Percent	Banks	Percent
Not important	4	80.0	1	50.0	3	100.0
Somewhat important	0	0.0	0	0.0	0	0.0
Very important	1	20.0	1	50.0	0	0.0
Total	5	100.0	2	100.0	3	100.0

g. Deterioration in your bank's current or expected liquidity position

	All Respondents		Large Banks		Other Banks	
	Banks	Percent	Banks	Percent	Banks	Percent
Not important	5	100.0	2	100.0	3	100.0
Somewhat important	0	0.0	0	0.0	0	0.0
Very important	0	0.0	0	0.0	0	0.0
Total	5	100.0	2	100.0	3	100.0

h. Increased concerns about the effects of legislative changes, supervisory actions, or changes in accounting standards

	All Respondents		Large Banks		Other Banks	
	Banks	Percent	Banks	Percent	Banks	Percent
Not important	3	60.0	2	100.0	1	33.3
Somewhat important	2	40.0	0	0.0	2	66.7
Very important	0	0.0	0	0.0	0	0.0
Total	5	100.0	2	100.0	3	100.0

B. Possible reasons for easing credit standards or loan terms:

a. Improvement in your bank's current or expected capital position

	All Respondents		Large Banks		Other Banks	
	Banks	Percent	Banks	Percent	Banks	Percent
Not important	40	90.9	21	91.3	19	90.5
Somewhat important	4	9.1	2	8.7	2	9.5
Very important	0	0.0	0	0.0	0	0.0
Total	44	100.0	23	100.0	21	100.0

b. More favorable or less uncertain economic outlook

	All Respondents		Large Banks		Other Banks	
	Banks	Percent	Banks	Percent	Banks	Percent
Not important	28	62.2	15	65.2	13	59.1
Somewhat important	15	33.3	7	30.4	8	36.4
Very important	2	4.4	1	4.3	1	4.5
Total	45	100.0	23	100.0	22	100.0

c. Improvement in industry-specific problems (please specify industries)

	All Respondents		Large Banks		Other Banks	
	Banks	Percent	Banks	Percent	Banks	Percent
Not important	39	86.7	23	100.0	16	72.7
Somewhat important	6	13.3	0	0.0	6	27.3
Very important	0	0.0	0	0.0	0	0.0
Total	45	100.0	23	100.0	22	100.0

d. More aggressive competition from other banks or nonbank lenders (other financial intermediaries or the capital markets)

	All Respondents		Large Banks		Other Banks	
	Banks	Percent	Banks	Percent	Banks	Percent
Not important	3	6.8	1	4.3	2	9.5
Somewhat important	6	13.6	3	13.0	3	14.3
Very important	35	79.5	19	82.6	16	76.2
Total	44	100.0	23	100.0	21	100.0

e. Increased tolerance for risk

	All Respondents		Large Banks		Other Banks	
	Banks	Percent	Banks	Percent	Banks	Percent
Not important	32	72.7	19	82.6	13	61.9
Somewhat important	12	27.3	4	17.4	8	38.1
Very important	0	0.0	0	0.0	0	0.0
Total	44	100.0	23	100.0	21	100.0

f. Increased liquidity in the secondary market for these loans

	All Respondents		Large Banks		Other Banks	
	Banks	Percent	Banks	Percent	Banks	Percent
Not important	38	86.4	19	82.6	19	90.5
Somewhat important	6	13.6	4	17.4	2	9.5
Very important	0	0.0	0	0.0	0	0.0
Total	44	100.0	23	100.0	21	100.0

g. Improvement in your bank's current or expected liquidity position

	All Respondents		Large Banks		Other Banks	
	Banks	Percent	Banks	Percent	Banks	Percent
Not important	40	90.9	20	87.0	20	95.2
Somewhat important	4	9.1	3	13.0	1	4.8
Very important	0	0.0	0	0.0	0	0.0
Total	44	100.0	23	100.0	21	100.0

h. Reduced concerns about the effects of legislative changes, supervisory actions, or changes in accounting standards

	All Respondents		Large Banks		Other Banks	
	Banks	Percent	Banks	Percent	Banks	Percent
Not important	42	95.5	22	95.7	20	95.2
Somewhat important	2	4.5	1	4.3	1	4.8
Very important	0	0.0	0	0.0	0	0.0
Total	44	100.0	23	100.0	21	100.0

4. Apart from normal seasonal variation, how has demand for C&I loans changed over the past three months? (Please consider only funds actually disbursed as opposed to requests for new or increased lines of credit.)

A. Demand for C&I loans from large and middle-market firms (annual sales of $50 million or more):

	All Respondents		Large Banks		Other Banks	
	Banks	Percent	Banks	Percent	Banks	Percent
Substantially stronger	0	0.0	0	0.0	0	0.0
Moderately stronger	20	26.3	11	27.5	9	25.0
About the same	48	63.2	26	65.0	22	61.1
Moderately weaker	8	10.5	3	7.5	5	13.9
Substantially weaker	0	0.0	0	0.0	0	0.0
Total	76	100.0	40	100.0	36	100.0

B. Demand for C&I loans from small firms (annual sales of less than $50 million):

	All Respondents		Large Banks		Other Banks	
	Banks	Percent	Banks	Percent	Banks	Percent
Substantially stronger	0	0.0	0	0.0	0	0.0
Moderately stronger	13	17.8	4	10.8	9	25.0
About the same	51	69.9	30	81.1	21	58.3
Moderately weaker	9	12.3	3	8.1	6	16.7
Substantially weaker	0	0.0	0	0.0	0	0.0
Total	73	100.0	37	100.0	36	100.0

5. If demand for C&I loans has strengthened or weakened over the past three months (as described in question 4), how important have been the following possible reasons for the change?

A. If stronger loan demand (answer 1 or 2 to question 4A or 4B), possible reasons:

a. Customer inventory financing needs increased

	All Respondents		Large Banks		Other Banks	
	Banks	Percent	Banks	Percent	Banks	Percent
Not important	5	25.0	4	40.0	1	10.0
Somewhat important	15	75.0	6	60.0	9	90.0
Very important	0	0.0	0	0.0	0	0.0
Total	20	100.0	10	100.0	10	100.0

b. Customer accounts receivable financing needs increased

	All Respondents		Large Banks		Other Banks	
	Banks	Percent	Banks	Percent	Banks	Percent
Not important	5	26.3	4	40.0	1	11.1
Somewhat important	14	73.7	6	60.0	8	88.9
Very important	0	0.0	0	0.0	0	0.0
Total	19	100.0	10	100.0	9	100.0

c. Customer investment in plant or equipment increased

	All Respondents		Large Banks		Other Banks	
	Banks	Percent	Banks	Percent	Banks	Percent
Not important	5	26.3	4	40.0	1	11.1
Somewhat important	13	68.4	6	60.0	7	77.8
Very important	1	5.3	0	0.0	1	11.1
Total	19	100.0	10	100.0	9	100.0

d. Customer internally generated funds decreased

	All Respondents		Large Banks		Other Banks	
	Banks	Percent	Banks	Percent	Banks	Percent
Not important	17	85.0	8	80.0	9	90.0
Somewhat important	3	15.0	2	20.0	1	10.0
Very important	0	0.0	0	0.0	0	0.0
Total	20	100.0	10	100.0	10	100.0

e. Customer merger or acquisition financing needs increased

	All Respondents		Large Banks		Other Banks	
	Banks	Percent	Banks	Percent	Banks	Percent
Not important	8	42.1	3	30.0	5	55.6
Somewhat important	6	31.6	2	20.0	4	44.4
Very important	5	26.3	5	50.0	0	0.0
Total	19	100.0	10	100.0	9	100.0

f. Customer borrowing shifted to your bank from other bank or nonbank sources because these other sources became less attractive

	All Respondents		Large Banks		Other Banks	
	Banks	Percent	Banks	Percent	Banks	Percent
Not important	9	47.4	6	60.0	3	33.3
Somewhat important	9	47.4	3	30.0	6	66.7
Very important	1	5.3	1	10.0	0	0.0
Total	19	100.0	10	100.0	9	100.0

g. Customers' precautionary demand for cash and liquidity increased

	All Respondents		Large Banks		Other Banks	
	Banks	Percent	Banks	Percent	Banks	Percent
Not important	19	100.0	10	100.0	9	100.0
Somewhat important	0	0.0	0	0.0	0	0.0
Very important	0	0.0	0	0.0	0	0.0
Total	19	100.0	10	100.0	9	100.0

B. If weaker loan demand (answer 4 or 5 to question 4A or 4B), possible reasons:

a. Customer inventory financing needs decreased

	All Respondents		Large Banks		Other Banks	
	Banks	Percent	Banks	Percent	Banks	Percent
Not important	7	77.8	3	100.0	4	66.7
Somewhat important	2	22.2	0	0.0	2	33.3
Very important	0	0.0	0	0.0	0	0.0
Total	9	100.0	3	100.0	6	100.0

b. Customer accounts receivable financing needs decreased

	All Respondents		Large Banks		Other Banks	
	Banks	Percent	Banks	Percent	Banks	Percent
Not important	6	66.7	3	100.0	3	50.0
Somewhat important	3	33.3	0	0.0	3	50.0
Very important	0	0.0	0	0.0	0	0.0
Total	9	100.0	3	100.0	6	100.0

c. Customer investment in plant or equipment decreased

	All Respondents		Large Banks		Other Banks	
	Banks	Percent	Banks	Percent	Banks	Percent
Not important	4	44.4	1	33.3	3	50.0
Somewhat important	5	55.6	2	66.7	3	50.0
Very important	0	0.0	0	0.0	0	0.0
Total	9	100.0	3	100.0	6	100.0

d. Customer internally generated funds increased

	All Respondents		Large Banks		Other Banks	
	Banks	Percent	Banks	Percent	Banks	Percent
Not important	4	44.4	0	0.0	4	66.7
Somewhat important	4	44.4	2	66.7	2	33.3
Very important	1	11.1	1	33.3	0	0.0
Total	9	100.0	3	100.0	6	100.0

e. Customer merger or acquisition financing needs decreased

	All Respondents		Large Banks		Other Banks	
	Banks	Percent	Banks	Percent	Banks	Percent
Not important	6	66.7	1	33.3	5	83.3
Somewhat important	3	33.3	2	66.7	1	16.7
Very important	0	0.0	0	0.0	0	0.0
Total	9	100.0	3	100.0	6	100.0

f. Customer borrowing shifted from your bank to other bank or nonbank sources because these other sources became more attractive

	All Respondents		Large Banks		Other Banks	
	Banks	Percent	Banks	Percent	Banks	Percent
Not important	5	55.6	2	66.7	3	50.0
Somewhat important	3	33.3	1	33.3	2	33.3
Very important	1	11.1	0	0.0	1	16.7
Total	9	100.0	3	100.0	6	100.0

g. Customers' precautionary demand for cash and liquidity decreased

	All Respondents		Large Banks		Other Banks	
	Banks	Percent	Banks	Percent	Banks	Percent
Not important	6	66.7	2	66.7	4	66.7
Somewhat important	3	33.3	1	33.3	2	33.3
Very important	0	0.0	0	0.0	0	0.0
Total	9	100.0	3	100.0	6	100.0

6. At your bank, apart from seasonal variation, how has the number of inquiries from potential business borrowers regarding the availability and terms of new credit lines or increases in existing lines changed over the past three months? (Please consider only inquiries for additional or increased C&I lines as opposed to the refinancing of existing loans.)

	All Respondents		Large Banks		Other Banks	
	Banks	Percent	Banks	Percent	Banks	Percent
The number of inquiries has increased substantially	0	0.0	0	0.0	0	0.0
The number of inquiries has increased moderately	19	25.0	10	25.0	9	25.0
The number of inquiries has stayed about the same	50	65.8	25	62.5	25	69.4
The number of inquiries has decreased moderately	7	9.2	5	12.5	2	5.6
The number of inquiries has decreased substantially	0	0.0	0	0.0	0	0.0
Total	76	100.0	40	100.0	36	100.0

*Evidence from Call Report data and other sources suggests that the rate of growth of banks' loans in the **retail small business lending category** (that is, bank loans to small businesses that are usually evaluated either with credit scores generated from an internally developed credit scoring model or with credit scores purchased from a vendor) has significantly lagged the recovery in C&I loans to larger businesses in recent years. Question 7 examines the recent annual volume of applications for these types of loans received by your bank relative to long-run averages. Question 8 examines your current underwriting policies for accepting applications for these types of loans relative to their long-run averages. Finally, question 9 asks about the expected change in the volume of your bank's new term loans and lines of credit to retail small businesses over the next twelve months.*

7. Please evaluate the total volume of applications for new *retail small business loans* that your bank received in the past year *(including both applications that resulted in a loan offer and those that did not)* as compared to the midpoint in the range between the highest and the lowest annual volumes of applications received at your bank over the past decade. Please consider the annual volume of applications for new term loans, for new lines of credit or for increases in credit limits on existing credit lines as well as for new business credit card loans or for increases in business credit card limits to retail small businesses. The annual volume of applications for new *retail small business loans* at my bank over the past year was:

	All Respondents		Large Banks		Other Banks	
	Banks	Percent	Banks	Percent	Banks	Percent
Substantially above the midpoint of the range that annual volumes of applications have been during this period	4	5.7	2	5.6	2	5.9
Moderately above the midpoint of the range that annual volumes of applications have been during this period	20	28.6	10	27.8	10	29.4
About the same as the midpoint of the range that annual volumes of applications have been during this period	23	32.9	12	33.3	11	32.4
Moderately below the midpoint of the range that annual volumes of applications have been during this period	14	20.0	9	25.0	5	14.7
Substantially below the midpoint of the range that annual volumes of applications have been during this period	5	7.1	2	5.6	3	8.8
My bank stopped originating such loans during this period	1	1.4	0	0.0	1	2.9
My bank has never originated such loans	3	4.3	1	2.8	2	5.9
Total	70	100.0	36	100.0	34	100.0

8. Please evaluate your current minimum underwriting policies for approving applications for new *retail small business loans* received by your bank *over the past year* for each of the following characteristics of the applications received and compare them to the midpoint of the range between the tightest and the easiest underwriting policies implemented by your bank over the past decade.

      a. Quality of collateral used

	All Respondents		Large Banks		Other Banks	
	Banks	Percent	Banks	Percent	Banks	Percent
near the easiest level that underwriting policies have been during this period	0	0.0	0	0.0	0	0.0
significantly easier than the midpoint of the range that underwriting policies have been during this period	1	1.5	1	2.9	0	0.0
somewhat easier than the midpoint of the range that underwriting policies have been during this period	7	10.6	4	11.8	3	9.4
near the midpoint than the midpoint of the range that underwriting policies have been during this period	46	69.7	25	73.5	21	65.6
somewhat tighter than the midpoint of the range that underwriting policies have been during this period	8	12.1	3	8.8	5	15.6
significantly tighter than the midpoint of the range that underwriting policies have been during this period	3	4.5	0	0.0	3	9.4
near the tightest level that underwriting policies have been during this period	1	1.5	1	2.9	0	0.0
Total	66	100.0	34	100.0	32	100.0

b. Quality of personal guarantees

	All Respondents		Large Banks		Other Banks	
	Banks	Percent	Banks	Percent	Banks	Percent
near the easiest level that underwriting policies have been during this period	0	0.0	0	0.0	0	0.0
significantly easier than the midpoint of the range that underwriting policies have been during this period	0	0.0	0	0.0	0	0.0
somewhat easier than the midpoint of the range that underwriting policies have been during this period	4	6.1	2	5.9	2	6.3
near the midpoint than the midpoint of the range that underwriting policies have been during this period	48	72.7	26	76.5	22	68.8
somewhat tighter than the midpoint of the range that underwriting policies have been during this period	9	13.6	4	11.8	5	15.6
significantly tighter than the midpoint of the range that underwriting policies have been during this period	4	6.1	1	2.9	3	9.4
near the tightest level that underwriting policies have been during this period	1	1.5	1	2.9	0	0.0
Total	66	100.0	34	100.0	32	100.0

c. Debt-to-income level of business owners

	All Respondents		Large Banks		Other Banks	
	Banks	Percent	Banks	Percent	Banks	Percent
near the easiest level that underwriting policies have been during this period	0	0.0	0	0.0	0	0.0
significantly easier than the midpoint of the range that underwriting policies have been during this period	0	0.0	0	0.0	0	0.0
somewhat easier than the midpoint of the range that underwriting policies have been during this period	4	6.2	3	8.8	1	3.2
near the midpoint than the midpoint of the range that underwriting policies have been during this period	48	73.8	23	67.6	25	80.6
somewhat tighter than the midpoint of the range that underwriting policies have been during this period	9	13.8	6	17.6	3	9.7
significantly tighter than the midpoint of the range that underwriting policies have been during this period	3	4.6	1	2.9	2	6.5
near the tightest level that underwriting policies have been during this period	1	1.5	1	2.9	0	0.0
Total	65	100.0	34	100.0	31	100.0

d. FICO scores of business owners

	All Respondents		Large Banks		Other Banks	
	Banks	Percent	Banks	Percent	Banks	Percent
near the easiest level that underwriting policies have been during this period	0	0.0	0	0.0	0	0.0
significantly easier than the midpoint of the range that underwriting policies have been during this period	0	0.0	0	0.0	0	0.0
somewhat easier than the midpoint of the range that underwriting policies have been during this period	7	10.9	4	11.8	3	10.0
near the midpoint than the midpoint of the range that underwriting policies have been during this period	42	65.6	21	61.8	21	70.0
somewhat tighter than the midpoint of the range that underwriting policies have been during this period	12	18.8	7	20.6	5	16.7
significantly tighter than the midpoint of the range that underwriting policies have been during this period	2	3.1	1	2.9	1	3.3
near the tightest level that underwriting policies have been during this period	1	1.6	1	2.9	0	0.0
Total	64	100.0	34	100.0	30	100.0

e. Liquidity position of business owners

	All Respondents		Large Banks		Other Banks	
	Banks	Percent	Banks	Percent	Banks	Percent
near the easiest level that underwriting policies have been during this period	0	0.0	0	0.0	0	0.0
significantly easier than the midpoint of the range that underwriting policies have been during this period	0	0.0	0	0.0	0	0.0
somewhat easier than the midpoint of the range that underwriting policies have been during this period	3	4.5	0	0.0	3	9.4
near the midpoint than the midpoint of the range that underwriting policies have been during this period	48	72.7	26	76.5	22	68.8
somewhat tighter than the midpoint of the range that underwriting policies have been during this period	12	18.2	7	20.6	5	15.6
significantly tighter than the midpoint of the range that underwriting policies have been during this period	2	3.0	0	0.0	2	6.3
near the tightest level that underwriting policies have been during this period	1	1.5	1	2.9	0	0.0
Total	66	100.0	34	100.0	32	100.0

f. Prospects for business growth or enterprise values

	All Respondents		Large Banks		Other Banks	
	Banks	Percent	Banks	Percent	Banks	Percent
near the easiest level that underwriting policies have been during this period	0	0.0	0	0.0	0	0.0
significantly easier than the midpoint of the range that underwriting policies have been during this period	0	0.0	0	0.0	0	0.0
somewhat easier than the midpoint of the range that underwriting policies have been during this period	4	6.1	2	5.9	2	6.3
near the midpoint than the midpoint of the range that underwriting policies have been during this period	50	75.8	26	76.5	24	75.0
somewhat tighter than the midpoint of the range that underwriting policies have been during this period	8	12.1	5	14.7	3	9.4
significantly tighter than the midpoint of the range that underwriting policies have been during this period	4	6.1	1	2.9	3	9.4
near the tightest level that underwriting policies have been during this period	0	0.0	0	0.0	0	0.0
Total	66	100.0	34	100.0	32	100.0

9. Assuming that the economy and financial markets evolve in line with consensus forecasts, how do you expect your bank's volume of originations of new term loans, new lines of credit or increases in limits on existing lines of credit to retail small businesses to change over the next twelve months? My bank expects that the provision of credit to retail small businesses over the *next twelve months* will:

	All Respondents		Large Banks		Other Banks	
	Banks	Percent	Banks	Percent	Banks	Percent
Increase substantially	2	2.9	1	2.9	1	2.9
Increase moderately	47	69.1	27	79.4	20	58.8
Remain about the same	18	26.5	6	17.6	12	35.3
Decrease moderately	1	1.5	0	0.0	1	2.9
Decrease substantially	0	0.0	0	0.0	0	0.0
Total	68	100.0	34	100.0	34	100.0

Questions 10-15 ask about changes in standards and demand over the **past three months** for three different types of CRE loans at your bank: construction and land development loans, loans secured by nonfarm nonresidential properties, and loans secured by multifamily residential properties. Please report changes in enforcement of existing policies as changes in policies.

10. Over the past three months, how have your bank's credit standards for approving new applications for construction and land development loans or credit lines changed?

	All Respondents		Large Banks		Other Banks	
	Banks	Percent	Banks	Percent	Banks	Percent
Tightened considerably	0	0.0	0	0.0	0	0.0
Tightened somewhat	1	1.4	1	2.6	0	0.0
Remained basically unchanged	64	86.5	31	81.6	33	91.7
Eased somewhat	9	12.2	6	15.8	3	8.3
Eased considerably	0	0.0	0	0.0	0	0.0
Total	74	100.0	38	100.0	36	100.0

11. Over the past three months, how have your bank's credit standards for approving new applications for loans secured by nonfarm nonresidential properties changed?

	All Respondents		Large Banks		Other Banks	
	Banks	Percent	Banks	Percent	Banks	Percent
Tightened considerably	0	0.0	0	0.0	0	0.0
Tightened somewhat	1	1.3	0	0.0	1	2.8
Remained basically unchanged	68	90.7	35	89.7	33	91.7
Eased somewhat	6	8.0	4	10.3	2	5.6
Eased considerably	0	0.0	0	0.0	0	0.0
Total	75	100.0	39	100.0	36	100.0

12. Over the past three months, how have your bank's credit standards for approving new applications for loans secured by multifamily residential properties changed?

	All Respondents		Large Banks		Other Banks	
	Banks	Percent	Banks	Percent	Banks	Percent
Tightened considerably	0	0.0	0	0.0	0	0.0
Tightened somewhat	9	12.0	4	10.3	5	13.9
Remained basically unchanged	58	77.3	27	69.2	31	86.1
Eased somewhat	8	10.7	8	20.5	0	0.0
Eased considerably	0	0.0	0	0.0	0	0.0
Total	75	100.0	39	100.0	36	100.0

13. Apart from normal seasonal variation, how has demand for construction and land development loans changed over the past three months? (Please consider the number of requests for new spot loans, for disbursement of funds under existing loan commitments, and for new or increased credit lines.)

	All Respondents		Large Banks		Other Banks	
	Banks	Percent	Banks	Percent	Banks	Percent
Substantially stronger	0	0.0	0	0.0	0	0.0
Moderately stronger	18	24.3	7	18.4	11	30.6
About the same	51	68.9	28	73.7	23	63.9
Moderately weaker	5	6.8	3	7.9	2	5.6
Substantially weaker	0	0.0	0	0.0	0	0.0
Total	74	100.0	38	100.0	36	100.0

14. Apart from normal seasonal variation, how has demand for loans secured by nonfarm nonresidential properties changed over the past three months? (Please consider the number of requests for new spot loans, for disbursement of funds under existing loan commitments, and for new or increased credit lines.)

	All Respondents		Large Banks		Other Banks	
	Banks	Percent	Banks	Percent	Banks	Percent
Substantially stronger	0	0.0	0	0.0	0	0.0
Moderately stronger	21	27.6	10	25.0	11	30.6
About the same	53	69.7	29	72.5	24	66.7
Moderately weaker	2	2.6	1	2.5	1	2.8
Substantially weaker	0	0.0	0	0.0	0	0.0
Total	76	100.0	40	100.0	36	100.0

15. Apart from normal seasonal variation, how has demand for loans secured by multifamily residential properties changed over the past three months? (Please consider the number of requests for new spot loans, for disbursement of funds under existing loan commitments, and for new or increased credit lines.)

	All Respondents		Large Banks		Other Banks	
	Banks	Percent	Banks	Percent	Banks	Percent
Substantially stronger	1	1.3	0	0.0	1	2.8
Moderately stronger	21	27.6	7	17.5	14	38.9
About the same	51	67.1	32	80.0	19	52.8
Moderately weaker	3	3.9	1	2.5	2	5.6
Substantially weaker	0	0.0	0	0.0	0	0.0
Total	76	100.0	40	100.0	36	100.0

Questions 16-17 *ask about three categories of **residential mortgage loans** at your bank—prime residential mortgages, nontraditional residential mortgages, and subprime residential mortgages. Question 16 deals with changes in your bank's credit standards for loans in each of these categories over the past three months. Question 17 deals with changes in demand for loans in each of these categories over the same period. If your bank's credit standards have not changed over the relevant period, please report them as unchanged even if the standards are either restrictive or accommodative relative to longer-term norms. If your bank's credit standards have tightened or eased over the relevant period, please so report them regardless of how they stand relative to longer-term norms. Also, please report changes in enforcement of existing standards as changes in standards.*

For the purposes of this survey, please use the following definitions of these loan categories (note that the loan categories are not mutually exclusive) and include first-lien loans only:

- *The **prime** category of residential mortgages includes loans made to borrowers that typically had relatively strong, well-documented credit histories, relatively high credit scores, and relatively low debt-to-income ratios at the time of origination. This would include fully amortizing loans that have a fixed rate, a standard adjustable rate, or a common hybrid adjustable rate—those for which the interest rate is initially fixed for a multi-year period and subsequently adjusts more frequently.*

- *The **nontraditional** category of residential mortgages includes, but is not limited to, adjustable-rate mortgages with multiple payment options, interest-only mortgages, and ``Alt-A'' products such as mortgages with limited income verification and mortgages secured by non-owner-occupied properties. (Please exclude standard adjustable-rate mortgages and common hybrid adjustable-rate mortgages.)*

- *The **subprime** category of residential mortgages typically includes loans made to borrowers that displayed one or more of the following characteristics at the time of origination: weakened credit histories that include payment delinquencies, chargeoffs, judgments, and/or bankruptcies; reduced repayment capacity as measured by credit scores or debt-to-income ratios; or incomplete credit histories.*

16. Over the past three months, how have your bank's credit standards for approving applications from individuals for mortgage loans to purchase homes changed?

A. Credit standards on mortgage loans that your bank categorizes as prime residential mortgages have:

	All Respondents		Large Banks		Other Banks	
	Banks	Percent	Banks	Percent	Banks	Percent
Tightened considerably	0	0.0	0	0.0	0	0.0
Tightened somewhat	2	2.8	0	0.0	2	5.6
Remained basically unchanged	60	83.3	27	75.0	33	91.7
Eased somewhat	10	13.9	9	25.0	1	2.8
Eased considerably	0	0.0	0	0.0	0	0.0
Total	72	100.0	36	100.0	36	100.0

B. Credit standards on mortgage loans that your bank categorizes as nontraditional residential mortgages have:

	All Respondents		Large Banks		Other Banks	
	Banks	Percent	Banks	Percent	Banks	Percent
Tightened considerably	1	2.9	0	0.0	1	6.7
Tightened somewhat	1	2.9	0	0.0	1	6.7
Remained basically unchanged	29	82.9	17	85.0	12	80.0
Eased somewhat	4	11.4	3	15.0	1	6.7
Eased considerably	0	0.0	0	0.0	0	0.0
Total	35	100.0	20	100.0	15	100.0

For this question, 36 respondent answered "My bank does not originate nontraditional residential mortgages."

C. Credit standards on mortgage loans that your bank categorizes as subprime residential mortgages have:

	All Respondents		Large Banks		Other Banks	
	Banks	Percent	Banks	Percent	Banks	Percent
Tightened considerably	0	0.0	0	0.0	0	0.0
Tightened somewhat	1	16.7	0	0.0	1	33.3
Remained basically unchanged	4	66.7	2	66.7	2	66.7
Eased somewhat	1	16.7	1	33.3	0	0.0
Eased considerably	0	0.0	0	0.0	0	0.0
Total	6	100.0	3	100.0	3	100.0

For this question, 62 respondents answered "My bank does not originate subprime residential mortgages."

17. Apart from normal seasonal variation, how has demand for mortgages to purchase homes changed over the past three months? (Please consider only new originations as opposed to the refinancing of existing mortgages.)

A. Demand for mortgages that your bank categorizes as prime residential mortgages was:

	All Respondents		Large Banks		Other Banks	
	Banks	Percent	Banks	Percent	Banks	Percent
Substantially stronger	0	0.0	0	0.0	0	0.0
Moderately stronger	14	19.4	4	11.1	10	27.8
About the same	43	59.7	22	61.1	21	58.3
Moderately weaker	15	20.8	10	27.8	5	13.9
Substantially weaker	0	0.0	0	0.0	0	0.0
Total	72	100.0	36	100.0	36	100.0

For this question, 1 respondent answered "My bank does not originate prime residential mortgages."

B. Demand for mortgages that your bank categorizes as nontraditional residential mortgages was:

	All Respondents		Large Banks		Other Banks	
	Banks	Percent	Banks	Percent	Banks	Percent
Substantially stronger	0	0.0	0	0.0	0	0.0
Moderately stronger	2	5.7	1	5.0	1	6.7
About the same	24	68.6	14	70.0	10	66.7
Moderately weaker	9	25.7	5	25.0	4	26.7
Substantially weaker	0	0.0	0	0.0	0	0.0
Total	35	100.0	20	100.0	15	100.0

For this question, 37 respondents answered "My bank does not originate nontraditional residential mortgages."

C. Demand for mortgages that your bank categorizes as subprime residential mortgages was:

	All Respondents		Large Banks		Other Banks	
	Banks	Percent	Banks	Percent	Banks	Percent
Substantially stronger	0	0.0	0	0.0	0	0.0
Moderately stronger	0	0.0	0	0.0	0	0.0
About the same	5	83.3	3	100.0	2	66.7
Moderately weaker	1	16.7	0	0.0	1	33.3
Substantially weaker	0	0.0	0	0.0	0	0.0
Total	6	100.0	3	100.0	3	100.0

For this question, 63 respondents answered "My bank does not originate subprime residential mortgages."

Questions 18-19 ask about **revolving home equity lines of credit** at your bank. *Question 18 deals with changes in your bank's credit standards over the past three months. Question 19 deals with changes in demand. If your bank's credit standards have not changed over the relevant period, please report them as unchanged even if they are either restrictive or accommodative relative to longer-term norms. If your bank's credit standards have tightened or eased over the relevant period, please so report them regardless of how they stand relative to longer-term norms. Also, please report changes in enforcement of existing standards as changes in standards.*

18. Over the past three months, how have your bank's credit standards for approving applications for revolving home equity lines of credit changed?

	All Respondents		Large Banks		Other Banks	
	Banks	Percent	Banks	Percent	Banks	Percent
Tightened considerably	0	0.0	0	0.0	0	0.0
Tightened somewhat	1	1.4	1	2.6	0	0.0
Remained basically unchanged	66	91.7	34	89.5	32	94.1
Eased somewhat	5	6.9	3	7.9	2	5.9
Eased considerably	0	0.0	0	0.0	0	0.0
Total	72	100.0	38	100.0	34	100.0

19. Apart from normal seasonal variation, how has demand for revolving home equity lines of credit changed over the past three months? (Please consider only funds actually disbursed as opposed to requests for new or increased lines of credit.)

	All Respondents		Large Banks		Other Banks	
	Banks	Percent	Banks	Percent	Banks	Percent
Substantially stronger	1	1.4	0	0.0	1	2.9
Moderately stronger	13	18.1	8	21.1	5	14.7
About the same	49	68.1	25	65.8	24	70.6
Moderately weaker	9	12.5	5	13.2	4	11.8
Substantially weaker	0	0.0	0	0.0	0	0.0
Total	72	100.0	38	100.0	34	100.0

Questions 20-29 ask about consumer lending at your bank. Question 20 deals with changes in your bank's willingness to make consumer loans over the past three months. Questions 21-26 deal with changes in credit standards and loan terms over the same period. Questions 27-29 deal with changes in demand for consumer loans over the past three months. If your bank's lending policies have not changed over the past three months, please report them as unchanged even if the policies are either restrictive or accommodative relative to longer-term norms. If your bank's policies have tightened or eased over the past three months, please so report them regardless of how they stand relative to longer-term norms. Also, please report changes in enforcement of existing policies as changes in policies.

20. Please indicate your bank's willingness to make consumer installment loans now as opposed to three months ago.

	All Respondents		Large Banks		Other Banks	
	Banks	Percent	Banks	Percent	Banks	Percent
Much more willing	0	0.0	0	0.0	0	0.0
Somewhat more willing	8	11.6	5	15.2	3	8.3
About unchanged	59	85.5	26	78.8	33	91.7
Somewhat less willing	2	2.9	2	6.1	0	0.0
Much less willing	0	0.0	0	0.0	0	0.0
Total	69	100.0	33	100.0	36	100.0

21. Over the past three months, how have your bank's credit standards for approving applications for credit cards from individuals or households changed?

	All Respondents		Large Banks		Other Banks	
	Banks	Percent	Banks	Percent	Banks	Percent
Tightened considerably	0	0.0	0	0.0	0	0.0
Tightened somewhat	0	0.0	0	0.0	0	0.0
Remained basically unchanged	52	91.2	29	90.6	23	92.0
Eased somewhat	5	8.8	3	9.4	2	8.0
Eased considerably	0	0.0	0	0.0	0	0.0
Total	57	100.0	32	100.0	25	100.0

22. Over the past three months, how have your bank's credit standards for approving applications for auto loans to individuals or households changed? (Please include loans arising from retail sales of passenger cars and other vehicles such as minivans, vans, sport-utility vehicles, pickup trucks, and similar light trucks for personal use, whether new or used. Please exclude loans to finance fleet sales, personal cash loans secured by automobiles already paid for, loans to finance the purchase of commercial vehicles and farm equipment, and lease financing.)

	All Respondents		Large Banks		Other Banks	
	Banks	Percent	Banks	Percent	Banks	Percent
Tightened considerably	0	0.0	0	0.0	0	0.0
Tightened somewhat	1	1.5	0	0.0	1	2.9
Remained basically unchanged	59	89.4	26	83.9	33	94.3
Eased somewhat	6	9.1	5	16.1	1	2.9
Eased considerably	0	0.0	0	0.0	0	0.0
Total	66	100.0	31	100.0	35	100.0

23. Over the past three months, how have your bank's credit standards for approving applications for consumer loans other than credit card and auto loans changed?

	All Respondents		Large Banks		Other Banks	
	Banks	Percent	Banks	Percent	Banks	Percent
Tightened considerably	0	0.0	0	0.0	0	0.0
Tightened somewhat	1	1.4	0	0.0	1	2.8
Remained basically unchanged	67	94.4	33	94.3	34	94.4
Eased somewhat	3	4.2	2	5.7	1	2.8
Eased considerably	0	0.0	0	0.0	0	0.0
Total	71	100.0	35	100.0	36	100.0

24. Over the past three months, how has your bank changed the following terms and conditions on new or existing credit card accounts for individuals or households?

a. Credit limits

	All Respondents		Large Banks		Other Banks	
	Banks	Percent	Banks	Percent	Banks	Percent
Tightened considerably	0	0.0	0	0.0	0	0.0
Tightened somewhat	1	1.9	1	3.3	0	0.0
Remained basically unchanged	46	88.5	25	83.3	21	95.5
Eased somewhat	5	9.6	4	13.3	1	4.5
Eased considerably	0	0.0	0	0.0	0	0.0
Total	52	100.0	30	100.0	22	100.0

b. Spreads of interest rates charged on outstanding balances over your bank's cost of funds (wider spreads=tightened, narrower spreads=eased)

	All Respondents		Large Banks		Other Banks	
	Banks	Percent	Banks	Percent	Banks	Percent
Tightened considerably	0	0.0	0	0.0	0	0.0
Tightened somewhat	3	5.8	2	6.7	1	4.5
Remained basically unchanged	47	90.4	27	90.0	20	90.9
Eased somewhat	2	3.8	1	3.3	1	4.5
Eased considerably	0	0.0	0	0.0	0	0.0
Total	52	100.0	30	100.0	22	100.0

c. Minimum percent of outstanding balances required to be repaid each month

	All Respondents		Large Banks		Other Banks	
	Banks	Percent	Banks	Percent	Banks	Percent
Tightened considerably	0	0.0	0	0.0	0	0.0
Tightened somewhat	2	3.8	1	3.3	1	4.5
Remained basically unchanged	50	96.2	29	96.7	21	95.5
Eased somewhat	0	0.0	0	0.0	0	0.0
Eased considerably	0	0.0	0	0.0	0	0.0
Total	52	100.0	30	100.0	22	100.0

d. Minimum required credit score (increased score=tightened, reduced score=eased)

	All Respondents		Large Banks		Other Banks	
	Banks	Percent	Banks	Percent	Banks	Percent
Tightened considerably	0	0.0	0	0.0	0	0.0
Tightened somewhat	0	0.0	0	0.0	0	0.0
Remained basically unchanged	48	92.3	27	90.0	21	95.5
Eased somewhat	4	7.7	3	10.0	1	4.5
Eased considerably	0	0.0	0	0.0	0	0.0
Total	52	100.0	30	100.0	22	100.0

e. The extent to which loans are granted to some customers that do not meet credit scoring thresholds (increased=eased, decreased=tightened)

	All Respondents		Large Banks		Other Banks	
	Banks	Percent	Banks	Percent	Banks	Percent
Tightened considerably	0	0.0	0	0.0	0	0.0
Tightened somewhat	0	0.0	0	0.0	0	0.0
Remained basically unchanged	50	96.2	29	96.7	21	95.5
Eased somewhat	2	3.8	1	3.3	1	4.5
Eased considerably	0	0.0	0	0.0	0	0.0
Total	52	100.0	30	100.0	22	100.0

25. Over the past three months, how has your bank changed the following terms and conditions on loans to individuals or households to purchase autos?

a. Maximum maturity

	All Respondents		Large Banks		Other Banks	
	Banks	Percent	Banks	Percent	Banks	Percent
Tightened considerably	0	0.0	0	0.0	0	0.0
Tightened somewhat	0	0.0	0	0.0	0	0.0
Remained basically unchanged	63	95.5	28	90.3	35	100.0
Eased somewhat	3	4.5	3	9.7	0	0.0
Eased considerably	0	0.0	0	0.0	0	0.0
Total	66	100.0	31	100.0	35	100.0

b. Spreads of loan rates over your bank's cost of funds (wider spreads=tightened, narrower spreads=eased)

	All Respondents		Large Banks		Other Banks	
	Banks	Percent	Banks	Percent	Banks	Percent
Tightened considerably	0	0.0	0	0.0	0	0.0
Tightened somewhat	7	10.6	6	19.4	1	2.9
Remained basically unchanged	53	80.3	23	74.2	30	85.7
Eased somewhat	6	9.1	2	6.5	4	11.4
Eased considerably	0	0.0	0	0.0	0	0.0
Total	66	100.0	31	100.0	35	100.0

c. Minimum required down payment (higher=tightened, lower=eased)

	All Respondents		Large Banks		Other Banks	
	Banks	Percent	Banks	Percent	Banks	Percent
Tightened considerably	0	0.0	0	0.0	0	0.0
Tightened somewhat	1	1.5	0	0.0	1	2.9
Remained basically unchanged	63	95.5	29	93.5	34	97.1
Eased somewhat	2	3.0	2	6.5	0	0.0
Eased considerably	0	0.0	0	0.0	0	0.0
Total	66	100.0	31	100.0	35	100.0

d. Minimum required credit score (increased score=tightened, reduced score=eased)

	All Respondents		Large Banks		Other Banks	
	Banks	Percent	Banks	Percent	Banks	Percent
Tightened considerably	0	0.0	0	0.0	0	0.0
Tightened somewhat	0	0.0	0	0.0	0	0.0
Remained basically unchanged	65	98.5	30	96.8	35	100.0
Eased somewhat	1	1.5	1	3.2	0	0.0
Eased considerably	0	0.0	0	0.0	0	0.0
Total	66	100.0	31	100.0	35	100.0

e. The extent to which loans are granted to some customers that do not meet credit scoring thresholds (increased=eased, decreased=tightened)

	All Respondents		Large Banks		Other Banks	
	Banks	Percent	Banks	Percent	Banks	Percent
Tightened considerably	0	0.0	0	0.0	0	0.0
Tightened somewhat	2	3.0	0	0.0	2	5.7
Remained basically unchanged	63	95.5	30	96.8	33	94.3
Eased somewhat	1	1.5	1	3.2	0	0.0
Eased considerably	0	0.0	0	0.0	0	0.0
Total	66	100.0	31	100.0	35	100.0

26. Over the past three months, how has your bank changed the following terms and conditions on consumer loans *other than* credit card and auto loans?

a. Maximum maturity

	All Respondents		Large Banks		Other Banks	
	Banks	Percent	Banks	Percent	Banks	Percent
Tightened considerably	0	0.0	0	0.0	0	0.0
Tightened somewhat	0	0.0	0	0.0	0	0.0
Remained basically unchanged	71	100.0	35	100.0	36	100.0
Eased somewhat	0	0.0	0	0.0	0	0.0
Eased considerably	0	0.0	0	0.0	0	0.0
Total	71	100.0	35	100.0	36	100.0

b. Spreads of loan rates over your bank's cost of funds (wider spreads=tightened, narrower spreads=eased)

	All Respondents		Large Banks		Other Banks	
	Banks	Percent	Banks	Percent	Banks	Percent
Tightened considerably	0	0.0	0	0.0	0	0.0
Tightened somewhat	1	1.4	0	0.0	1	2.8
Remained basically unchanged	65	91.5	33	94.3	32	88.9
Eased somewhat	5	7.0	2	5.7	3	8.3
Eased considerably	0	0.0	0	0.0	0	0.0
Total	71	100.0	35	100.0	36	100.0

c. Minimum required down payment (higher=tightened, lower=eased)

	All Respondents		Large Banks		Other Banks	
	Banks	Percent	Banks	Percent	Banks	Percent
Tightened considerably	0	0.0	0	0.0	0	0.0
Tightened somewhat	0	0.0	0	0.0	0	0.0
Remained basically unchanged	70	98.6	34	97.1	36	100.0
Eased somewhat	1	1.4	1	2.9	0	0.0
Eased considerably	0	0.0	0	0.0	0	0.0
Total	71	100.0	35	100.0	36	100.0

d. Minimum required credit score (increased score=tightened, reduced score=eased)

	All Respondents		Large Banks		Other Banks	
	Banks	Percent	Banks	Percent	Banks	Percent
Tightened considerably	0	0.0	0	0.0	0	0.0
Tightened somewhat	0	0.0	0	0.0	0	0.0
Remained basically unchanged	69	97.2	34	97.1	35	97.2
Eased somewhat	2	2.8	1	2.9	1	2.8
Eased considerably	0	0.0	0	0.0	0	0.0
Total	71	100.0	35	100.0	36	100.0

e. The extent to which loans are granted to some customers that do not meet credit scoring thresholds (increased=eased, decreased=tightened)

	All Respondents		Large Banks		Other Banks	
	Banks	Percent	Banks	Percent	Banks	Percent
Tightened considerably	0	0.0	0	0.0	0	0.0
Tightened somewhat	2	2.9	1	2.9	1	2.8
Remained basically unchanged	67	95.7	33	97.1	34	94.4
Eased somewhat	1	1.4	0	0.0	1	2.8
Eased considerably	0	0.0	0	0.0	0	0.0
Total	70	100.0	34	100.0	36	100.0

27. Apart from normal seasonal variation, how has demand from individuals or households for credit card loans changed over the past three months?

	All Respondents		Large Banks		Other Banks	
	Banks	Percent	Banks	Percent	Banks	Percent
Substantially stronger	0	0.0	0	0.0	0	0.0
Moderately stronger	7	13.7	5	16.7	2	9.5
About the same	41	80.4	23	76.7	18	85.7
Moderately weaker	3	5.9	2	6.7	1	4.8
Substantially weaker	0	0.0	0	0.0	0	0.0
Total	51	100.0	30	100.0	21	100.0

28. Apart from normal seasonal variation, how has demand from individuals or households for auto loans changed over the past three months?

	All Respondents		Large Banks		Other Banks	
	Banks	Percent	Banks	Percent	Banks	Percent
Substantially stronger	0	0.0	0	0.0	0	0.0
Moderately stronger	22	32.8	12	37.5	10	28.6
About the same	40	59.7	17	53.1	23	65.7
Moderately weaker	5	7.5	3	9.4	2	5.7
Substantially weaker	0	0.0	0	0.0	0	0.0
Total	67	100.0	32	100.0	35	100.0

29. Apart from normal seasonal variation, how has demand from individuals or households for consumer loans other than credit card and auto loans changed over the past three months?

	All Respondents		Large Banks		Other Banks	
	Banks	Percent	Banks	Percent	Banks	Percent
Substantially stronger	0	0.0	0	0.0	0	0.0
Moderately stronger	9	12.5	2	5.6	7	19.4
About the same	60	83.3	32	88.9	28	77.8
Moderately weaker	3	4.2	2	5.6	1	2.8
Substantially weaker	0	0.0	0	0.0	0	0.0
Total	72	100.0	36	100.0	36	100.0

*According to the Call Reports, auto loans at banks have grown rapidly this year. Questions 30-31 ask you to compare your bank's current policies on approving applications for auto loans that your bank characterizes as **subprime** with the stance of those policies a year ago. Question 32 asks about how you expect lending policies for auto loans categorized by your bank as subprime to change at your institution over the next year. (Please consider only loans to individuals and households and report changes in enforcement of existing policies as changes in policies)*

30. Over the past twelve months, how has your bank changed the following terms on the **subprime** category of auto loans for the purchase of new or used autos?

a. Maximum maturity (longer maturity eased, shorter maturity tightened)

	All Respondents		Large Banks		Other Banks	
	Banks	Percent	Banks	Percent	Banks	Percent
tightened considerably	0	0.0	0	0.0	0	0.0
tightened somewhat	2	10.5	0	0.0	2	16.7
remained basically unchanged	16	84.2	6	85.7	10	83.3
eased somewhat	1	5.3	1	14.3	0	0.0
eased considerably	0	0.0	0	0.0	0	0.0
Total	19	100.0	7	100.0	12	100.0

For this question, 40 respondents answered "my bank does not originate subprime auto loans."

b. Spreads of loan rates over your bank's cost of funds (wider spreads tightened, narrower spreads eased)

	All Respondents		Large Banks		Other Banks	
	Banks	Percent	Banks	Percent	Banks	Percent
tightened considerably	0	0.0	0	0.0	0	0.0
tightened somewhat	1	5.3	1	14.3	0	0.0
remained basically unchanged	16	84.2	4	57.1	12	100.0
eased somewhat	2	10.5	2	28.6	0	0.0
eased considerably	0	0.0	0	0.0	0	0.0
Total	19	100.0	7	100.0	12	100.0

For this question, 40 respondents answered "my bank does not originate subprime auto loans."

c. Minimum required down payment (higher tightened, lower eased)

	All Respondents		Large Banks		Other Banks	
	Banks	Percent	Banks	Percent	Banks	Percent
tightened considerably	0	0.0	0	0.0	0	0.0
tightened somewhat	1	5.3	0	0.0	1	8.3
remained basically unchanged	15	78.9	6	85.7	9	75.0
eased somewhat	3	15.8	1	14.3	2	16.7
eased considerably	0	0.0	0	0.0	0	0.0
Total	19	100.0	7	100.0	12	100.0

For this question, 40 respondents answered "my bank does not originate subprime auto loans."

d. Minimum required credit score (higher score tightened, lower score eased)

	All Respondents		Large Banks		Other Banks	
	Banks	Percent	Banks	Percent	Banks	Percent
tightened considerably	0	0.0	0	0.0	0	0.0
tightened somewhat	1	5.3	0	0.0	1	8.3
remained basically unchanged	17	89.5	7	100.0	10	83.3
eased somewhat	1	5.3	0	0.0	1	8.3
eased considerably	0	0.0	0	0.0	0	0.0
Total	19	100.0	7	100.0	12	100.0

For this question, 40 respondents answered "my bank does not originate subprime auto loans."

31. If your bank has tightened or eased any of its terms on the subprime category of auto loans for the purchase of new or used cars over the past *twelve months,* how important have been the following possible reasons for the change?

A. Possible reasons for tightening terms over the past twelve months (answered 1 or 2 to any of a, b, c or d in question 30):

a. Deterioration in your bank's current or expected capital or liquidity position

Responses are not reported when the number of respondents is 3 or fewer

b. Less favorable or more uncertain economic outlook

Responses are not reported when the number of respondents is 3 or fewer

c. Less aggressive competition from other banks or nonbank lenders

Responses are not reported when the number of respondents is 3 or fewer

e. Decreased liquidity in the secondary market for these loans

Responses are not reported when the number of respondents is 3 or fewer

f. Decreased or more uncertain collateral values

Responses are not reported when the number of respondents is 3 or fewer

g. Deterioration in performance of recently originated loans

Responses are not reported when the number of respondents is 3 or fewer

h. Deterioration in relationship with auto dealers who originate loans

Responses are not reported when the number of respondents is 3 or fewer

i. Average duration of auto loans has become less favorable

Responses are not reported when the number of respondents is 3 or fewer

B. Possible reasons for easing terms over the past twelve months (answered 4 or 5 to any of a, b, c or d in question 30):

a. Improvement in your bank's current or expected capital or liquidity position

	All Respondents		Large Banks		Other Banks	
	Banks	Percent	Banks	Percent	Banks	Percent
not important	4	100.0	3	100.0	1	100.0
somewhat important	0	0.0	0	0.0	0	0.0
very important	0	0.0	0	0.0	0	0.0
Total	4	100.0	3	100.0	1	100.0

b. More favorable or less uncertain economic outlook

	All Respondents		Large Banks		Other Banks	
	Banks	Percent	Banks	Percent	Banks	Percent
not important	3	75.0	3	100.0	0	0.0
somewhat important	1	25.0	0	0.0	1	100.0
very important	0	0.0	0	0.0	0	0.0
Total	4	100.0	3	100.0	1	100.0

c. More aggressive competition from other banks or nonbank lenders

	All Respondents		Large Banks		Other Banks	
	Banks	Percent	Banks	Percent	Banks	Percent
not important	0	0.0	0	0.0	0	0.0
somewhat important	3	75.0	2	66.7	1	100.0
very important	1	25.0	1	33.3	0	0.0
Total	4	100.0	3	100.0	1	100.0

d. Increased tolerance for risk

	All Respondents		Large Banks		Other Banks	
	Banks	Percent	Banks	Percent	Banks	Percent
not important	2	50.0	2	66.7	0	0.0
somewhat important	1	25.0	1	33.3	0	0.0
very important	1	25.0	0	0.0	1	100.0
Total	4	100.0	3	100.0	1	100.0

e. Increased liquidity in the secondary market for these loans

	All Respondents		Large Banks		Other Banks	
	Banks	Percent	Banks	Percent	Banks	Percent
not important	4	100.0	3	100.0	1	100.0
somewhat important	0	0.0	0	0.0	0	0.0
very important	0	0.0	0	0.0	0	0.0
Total	4	100.0	3	100.0	1	100.0

f. Increased or less uncertain collateral values

	All Respondents		Large Banks		Other Banks	
	Banks	Percent	Banks	Percent	Banks	Percent
not important	4	80.0	3	100.0	1	50.0
somewhat important	1	20.0	0	0.0	1	50.0
very important	0	0.0	0	0.0	0	0.0
Total	5	100.0	3	100.0	2	100.0

g. Improvement in the performance of recently originated loans

	All Respondents		Large Banks		Other Banks	
	Banks	Percent	Banks	Percent	Banks	Percent
not important	1	25.0	1	33.3	0	0.0
somewhat important	2	50.0	2	66.7	0	0.0
very important	1	25.0	0	0.0	1	100.0
Total	4	100.0	3	100.0	1	100.0

h. Improvement in relationship with auto dealers who originate loans

	All Respondents		Large Banks		Other Banks	
	Banks	Percent	Banks	Percent	Banks	Percent
not important	3	75.0	3	100.0	0	0.0
somewhat important	0	0.0	0	0.0	0	0.0
very important	1	25.0	0	0.0	1	100.0
Total	4	100.0	3	100.0	1	100.0

i. Average duration of auto loans has become more favorable

	All Respondents		Large Banks		Other Banks	
	Banks	Percent	Banks	Percent	Banks	Percent
not important	3	75.0	3	100.0	0	0.0
somewhat important	1	25.0	0	0.0	1	100.0
very important	0	0.0	0	0.0	0	0.0
Total	4	100.0	3	100.0	1	100.0

32. Assuming that the economy and financial markets evolve in line with consensus forecasts, how do you expect your bank's standards or terms for approving applications for the subprime category of auto loans for the purchase of *new or used autos* to change over the *next twelve months* ?

	All Respondents		Large Banks		Other Banks	
	Banks	Percent	Banks	Percent	Banks	Percent
Standards or terms will be tightened considerably	0	0.0	0	0.0	0	0.0
Standards or terms will be tightened somewhat	1	4.0	1	9.1	0	0.0
Standards or terms will remain basically unchanged	22	88.0	9	81.8	13	92.9
Standards or terms will be eased somewhat	2	8.0	1	9.1	1	7.1
Standards or terms will be eased considerably	0	0.0	0	0.0	0	0.0
Total	25	100.0	11	100.0	14	100.0

1. The sample is selected from among the largest banks in each Federal Reserve District. In the table, large banks are defined as those with total domestic assets of $20 billion or more as of June 30, 2014. The combined assets of the 40 large banks totaled $8.5 trillion, compared to $8.8 trillion for the entire panel of 76 banks, and $12.4 trillion for all domestically chartered, federally insured commercial banks.

Return to text

Senior Loan Officer Opinion Survey release dates | Surveys and reports

Home | Publications and reports | Economic research and data
Accessibility | Contact Us
Last update: November 3, 2014

Table 2

Senior Loan Officer Opinion Survey on Bank Lending Practices at Selected Branches and Agencies of Foreign Banks in the United States [1]

(Status of policy as of October 2014)

Questions 1-6 ask about commercial and industrial (C&I) loans at your bank. Questions 1-3 deal with changes in your bank's lending policies over the past three months. Questions 4-5 deal with changes in demand for C&I loans over the past three months. Question 6 asks about changes in prospective demand for C&I loans at your bank, as indicated by the volume of recent inquiries about the availability of new credit lines or increases in existing lines. If your bank's lending policies have not changed over the past three months, please report them as unchanged even if the policies are either restrictive or accommodative relative to longer-term norms. If your bank's policies have tightened or eased over the past three months, please so report them regardless of how they stand relative to longer-term norms. Also, please report changes in enforcement of existing policies as changes in policies.

1. Over the past three months, how have your bank's credit standards for approving applications for C&I loans or credit lines—other than those to be used to finance mergers and acquisitions—changed?

	All Respondents	
	Banks	Percent
Tightened considerably	0	0.0
Tightened somewhat	0	0.0
Remained basically unchanged	21	95.5
Eased somewhat	1	4.5
Eased considerably	0	0.0
Total	22	100.0

2. For applications for C&I loans or credit lines—other than those to be used to finance mergers and acquisitions—that your bank currently is willing to approve, how have the terms of those loans changed over the past three months?

a. Maximum size of credit lines

	All Respondents	
	Banks	Percent
Tightened considerably	0	0.0
Tightened somewhat	0	0.0
Remained basically unchanged	21	95.5
Eased somewhat	1	4.5
Eased considerably	0	0.0
Total	22	100.0

b. Maximum maturity of loans or credit lines

	All Respondents	
	Banks	Percent
Tightened considerably	0	0.0
Tightened somewhat	0	0.0
Remained basically unchanged	22	100.0
Eased somewhat	0	0.0
Eased considerably	0	0.0
Total	22	100.0

c. Costs of credit lines

	All Respondents	
	Banks	Percent
Tightened considerably	0	0.0
Tightened somewhat	1	4.5
Remained basically unchanged	20	90.9
Eased somewhat	1	4.5
Eased considerably	0	0.0
Total	22	100.0

d. Spreads of loan rates over your bank's cost of funds (wider spreads=tightened, narrower spreads=eased)

	All Respondents	
	Banks	Percent
Tightened considerably	0	0.0
Tightened somewhat	1	4.5
Remained basically unchanged	18	81.8
Eased somewhat	3	13.6
Eased considerably	0	0.0
Total	22	100.0

e. Premiums charged on riskier loans

	All Respondents	
	Banks	Percent
Tightened considerably	0	0.0
Tightened somewhat	1	4.5
Remained basically unchanged	20	90.9
Eased somewhat	1	4.5
Eased considerably	0	0.0
Total	22	100.0

f. Loan covenants

	All Respondents	
	Banks	Percent
Tightened considerably	0	0.0
Tightened somewhat	0	0.0
Remained basically unchanged	19	86.4
Eased somewhat	3	13.6
Eased considerably	0	0.0
Total	22	100.0

g. Collateralization requirements

	All Respondents	
	Banks	Percent
Tightened considerably	0	0.0
Tightened somewhat	1	4.5
Remained basically unchanged	21	95.5
Eased somewhat	0	0.0
Eased considerably	0	0.0
Total	22	100.0

h. Use of interest rate floors (more use=tightened, less use=eased)

	All Respondents	
	Banks	Percent
Tightened considerably	0	0.0
Tightened somewhat	0	0.0
Remained basically unchanged	19	100.0
Eased somewhat	0	0.0
Eased considerably	0	0.0
Total	19	100.0

3. If your bank has tightened or eased its credit standards or its terms for C&I loans or credit lines over the past three months (as described in questions 1 and 2), how important have been the following possible reasons for the change?

A. Possible reasons for tightening credit standards or loan terms:

a. Deterioration in your bank's current or expected capital position

Responses are not reported when the number of respondends is 3 or fewer

b. Less favorable or more uncertain economic outlook

Responses are not reported when the number of respondends is 3 or fewer

c. Worsening of industry-specific problems (please specify industries)

	All Respondents	
	Banks	Percent
Not important	0	--
Somewhat important	0	--
Very important	0	--
Total	0	--

d. Less aggressive competition from other banks or nonbank lenders (other financial intermediaries or the capital markets)

	All Respondents	
	Banks	Percent
Not important	0	--
Somewhat important	0	--
Very important	0	--
Total	0	--

e. Reduced tolerance for risk

Responses are not reported when the number of respondends is 3 or fewer

f. Decreased liquidity in the secondary market for these loans

	All Respondents	
	Banks	Percent
Not important	0	--
Somewhat important	0	--
Very important	0	--
Total	0	--

g. Deterioration in your bank's current or expected liquidity position

	All Respondents	
	Banks	Percent
Not important	0	--
Somewhat important	0	--
Very important	0	--
Total	0	--

h. Increased concerns about the potential effects of legislative changes, supervisory actions, or accounting standards

	All Respondents	
	Banks	Percent
Not important	0	--
Somewhat important	0	--
Very important	0	--
Total	0	--

B. Possible reasons for easing credit standards or loan terms:

a. Improvement in your bank's current or expected capital position

Responses are not reported when the number of respondends is 3 or fewer

b. More favorable or less uncertain economic outlook

	All Respondents	
	Banks	Percent
Not important	2	50.0
Somewhat important	2	50.0
Very important	0	0.0
Total	4	100.0

c. Improvement in industry-specific problems (please specify industries)

Responses are not reported when the number of respondends is 3 or fewer

d. More aggressive competition from other banks or nonbank lenders (other financial intermediaries or the capital markets)

	All Respondents	
	Banks	Percent
Not important	0	0.0
Somewhat important	1	25.0
Very important	3	75.0
Total	4	100.0

e. Increased tolerance for risk

	All Respondents	
	Banks	Percent
Not important	2	50.0
Somewhat important	2	50.0
Very important	0	0.0
Total	4	100.0

f. Increased liquidity in the secondary market for these loans

	All Respondents	
	Banks	Percent
Not important	2	50.0
Somewhat important	2	50.0
Very important	0	0.0
Total	4	100.0

g. Improvement in your bank's current or expected liquidity position

Responses are not reported when the number of respondends is 3 or fewer

h. Reduced concerns about the potential effects of legislative changes, supervisory actions, or accounting standards

	All Respondents	
	Banks	Percent
Not important	3	75.0
Somewhat important	1	25.0
Very important	0	0.0
Total	4	100.0

4. Apart from normal seasonal variation, how has demand for C&I loans changed over the past three months? (Please consider only funds actually disbursed as opposed to requests for new or increased lines of credit.)

	All Respondents	
	Banks	Percent
Substantially stronger	0	0.0
Moderately stronger	5	23.8
About the same	16	76.2
Moderately weaker	0	0.0
Substantially weaker	0	0.0
Total	21	100.0

5. If demand for C&I loans has strengthened or weakened over the past three months (as described in question 4), how important have been the following possible reasons for the change?

A. If stronger loan demand (answer 1 or 2 to question 4), possible reasons:

a. Customer inventory financing needs increased

	All Respondents	
	Banks	Percent
Not important	2	40.0
Somewhat important	3	60.0
Very important	0	0.0
Total	5	100.0

b. Customer accounts receivable financing needs increased

	All Respondents	
	Banks	Percent
Not important	3	60.0
Somewhat important	2	40.0
Very important	0	0.0
Total	5	100.0

c. Customer investment in plant or equipment increased

	All Respondents	
	Banks	Percent
Not important	3	60.0
Somewhat important	2	40.0
Very important	0	0.0
Total	5	100.0

d. Customer internally generated funds decreased

	All Respondents	
	Banks	Percent
Not important	4	80.0
Somewhat important	1	20.0
Very important	0	0.0
Total	5	100.0

e. Customer merger or acquisition financing needs increased

	All Respondents	
	Banks	Percent
Not important	2	40.0
Somewhat important	2	40.0
Very important	1	20.0
Total	5	100.0

f. Customer borrowing shifted to your bank from other bank or nonbank sources because these other sources became less attractive

	All Respondents	
	Banks	Percent
Not important	5	100.0
Somewhat important	0	0.0
Very important	0	0.0
Total	5	100.0

g. Customers' precautionary demand for cash and liquidity increased

	All Respondents	
	Banks	Percent
Not important	3	60.0
Somewhat important	2	40.0
Very important	0	0.0
Total	5	100.0

B. If weaker loan demand (answer 4 or 5 to question 4), possible reasons:

a. Customer inventory financing needs decreased

No responses were received for this question

b. Customer accounts receivable financing needs decreased

No responses were received for this question

c. Customer investment in plant or equipment decreased

No responses were received for this question

d. Customer internally generated funds increased

No responses were received for this question

e. Customer merger or acquisition financing needs decreased

No responses were received for this question

f. Customer borrowing shifted from your bank to other bank or nonbank sources because these other sources became more attractive

No responses were received for this question

g. Customers' precautionary demand for cash and liquidity decreased

No responses were received for this question

6. At your bank, apart from normal seasonal variation, how has the number of inquiries from potential business borrowers regarding the availability and terms of new credit lines or increases in existing lines changed over the past three months? (Please consider only inquiries for additional or increased C&I lines as opposed to the refinancing of existing loans.)

	All Respondents	
	Banks	Percent
The number of inquiries has increased substantially	0	0.0
The number of inquiries has increased moderately	5	22.7
The number of inquiries has stayed about the same	16	72.7
The number of inquiries has decreased moderately	1	4.5
The number of inquiries has decreased substantially	0	0.0
Total	22	100.0

Questions 7-8 *ask about commercial real estate (CRE) loans at your bank, including construction and land development loans and loans secured by nonfarm nonresidential real estate. Question 7 deals with changes in your bank's standards over the past three months. Question 8 deals with changes in demand. If your bank's lending standards or terms have not changed over the relevant period, please report them as unchanged even if they are either restrictive or accommodative relative to longer-term norms. If your bank's standards or terms have tightened or eased over the relevant period, please so report them regardless of how they stand relative to longer-term norms. Also, please report changes in enforcement of existing standards as changes in standards.*

7. Over the past three months, how have your bank's credit standards for approving applications for CRE loans changed?

	All Respondents	
	Banks	Percent
Tightened considerably	0	0.0
Tightened somewhat	0	0.0
Remained basically unchanged	10	83.3
Eased somewhat	2	16.7
Eased considerably	0	0.0
Total	12	100.0

8. Apart from normal seasonal variation, how has demand for CRE loans changed over the past three months?

	All Respondents	
	Banks	Percent
Substantially stronger	1	8.3
Moderately stronger	4	33.3
About the same	6	50.0
Moderately weaker	1	8.3
Substantially weaker	0	0.0
Total	12	100.0

1. As of June 30, 2014, the 22 respondents had combined assets of $1.4 trillion, compared to $2.6 trillion for all foreign related banking institutions in the United States. The sample is selected from among the largest foreign-related banking institutions in those Federal Reserve Districts where such institutions are common.
Return to text